DRAFTING, INTERPRETING, AND APPLYING LEGISLATION

OTHER BOOKS IN THE COLLECTION

Political Law in Canada

Canada's Parliament: A Primer

The Senate of Canada

The Recognition of Two Official Languages in Canada

Federalism in Canada: Evolving Constitutional, Political, and Social Realities

UNDERSTANDING CANADA

DRAFTING, INTERPRETING, AND APPLYING LEGISLATION

John Mark Keyes & Wendy Gordon

INSTITUTE OF PARLIAMENTARY AND POLITICAL LAW
INSTITUT DE DROIT PARLEMENTAIRE ET POLITIQUE

Drafting, Interpreting, and Applying Legislation

Published in 2023 by
Irwin Law Inc
Suite 206, 14 Duncan Street
Toronto, Ontario M5H 3G8
irwinlaw.com

Cover image: Adobe Stock

ISBN: 978-1-55221-681-1 | e-book ISBN: 978-1-55221-682-8

Cataloguing in Publication available from Library and Archives Canada

Title: Drafting, interpreting, and applying legislation / John Mark Keyes & Wendy Gordon.
Names: Keyes, John Mark, 1955– author. | Gordon, Wendy (Lawyer), author.
Description: Series statement: Understanding Canada | Includes bibliographical references and index.
Identifiers: Canadiana (print) 20230210465 | Canadiana (ebook) 20230215092 | ISBN 9781552216811 (softcover) | ISBN 9781552216828 (PDF)
Subjects: LCSH: Bill drafting — Canada. | LCSH: Law — Canada — Interpretation and construction.
Classification: LCC KE4560 .K49 2023 | LCC KF385.K73 K39 2023 kfmod | DDC 328.713/73—dc23

Printed and bound by CPI Group (UK) Ltd, Croydon, CR0 4YY
1 2 3 4 5 27 26 25 24 23

Contents

Foreword

A modern Democratic jurisdiction that aspires to rely on the rule of law in its system of governance must have a system of laws. In the Canadian context, the most prominently palpable component of the legal system is legislation; that is, the laws enacted by the federal Parliament, by the provincial and territorial legislatures, and by their delegates in the Executive Branch and in municipal institutions. This book deals with such laws as a primary instrument of governance.

Informed readers should focus first on the scope of this volume. John Mark Keyes and Wendy Gordon have charted here a complete life cycle of legislation. It begins by discussing what legislation is and what it does, as well as the purposes for which it is used. It then addresses the drafting of legislative texts and the processes for transforming them into law. It goes on to explain how legislation is found, understood, and applied, including the interpretive principles and techniques for resolving disputes about its meaning and application. Among the works dealing with the Canadian system of written laws, it is one of the most comprehensive in scope, encompassing both how legislation is made and how it is interpreted and applied.

The scope of the treatment of the subject matter in this book leads us to its actual and potential uses. Its utility for law students and legal practitioners is self-evident. Legislative drafting as a specialized branch of the practice of law may not be glorified in television shows, as criminal law and corporate law are. However, were it not for legislation, there would be no modern criminal law or corporate law. Generating legislation and knowing how to use it is just as important and equally interesting.

The understanding of legislation, as well as of its use in statecraft, is a central part of both public service and politics. A great deal of government and governing consists of the various uses and applications of legislation, along with updating it to keep pace with changing social needs and conditions. Familiarity with the path of legislation is a professional requirement for those working in the political sphere or in public administration, despite being seldom addressed in university programs. In a similar vein, in a Democracy, familiarization with both the path and the content of legislation are vital requisites for citizens to be well-informed about the law that applies to them. The expression "there ought to be a law" may constitute rhetorical usage, but it is grounded in the reality that a profession exists that is vital to bringing this saying to life.

Perhaps the most profound line of inquiry Keyes and Gordon draw us toward is to see whether drafting, enacting, and interpreting legislation is an art or a science. Undeniably, in the sense that the preparation and application of laws form part of a social discipline, we are in the realm of a social science. There are rules and processes to follow by which the political-legal system must abide. However, legislated law is not mechanical, and it is certainly not static. Rather, seen in its proper light, legislation expresses both the current organization and the collective aspirations, hopes, dreams, and even fears of Democratic society. In that sense, both as to content and form, legislation is a social and societal art of the highest order.

In sum, understanding legislation and how it is made is vital to grasping the Democratic nature of Canada.

Gregory Tardi, DJur
Editor, *Understanding Canada* collection
August 2022

Introduction

What Is This Book About?

This book is about an important type of law in Canada: *legislation*. It operates as part of Canada's legal system along with other types of law, such as common law, international law, parliamentary law, and Indigenous legal traditions. These various types of law operate together to make up the legal system that governs people in Canada.

The book is divided into two parts.

Part One, comprising chapters 1 to 3, describes how legislation is written ("drafted") and given the force of law ("enacted"). This introduction provides a general overview of what legislation is and what it does within the legal system. It forms the basis for a detailed consideration of how legislation comes into being as the product of an activity called "drafting" (Chapter One: What Is Drafting?) that is carried out in particular ways (Chapter Two: How Is Legislation Drafted?). The following chapter looks at how draft legislation is transformed into law (Chapter Three: How Is Draft Legislation Turned Into Law?).

Part Two, comprising chapters 4 to 9, considers how, once transformed into law, legislation functions within Canada's legal system. It begins with an account of how it operates generally (Chapter Four: What Is Legislation Used For? and Chapter Five: How Is Legislation

Interpreted and Applied?). It then examines in some detail three groups of matters Canadian courts focus on when interpreting and applying legislation (Chapter Six: Legislative Text, Chapter Seven: Purposes, and Chapter Eight: Context). Finally, this part looks at particular considerations relating to the application of legislation (Chapter Nine: Application).

These chapters address matters of fundamental importance to the operation of Canada's legal system. Whether legislation is understood and applied as its law-maker intended depends largely on the clarity with which the legislation is drafted, but is also influenced by the methodology used to understand and apply it.

The footnotes and bibliography provide suggestions for further reading for those who are interested in exploring these matters in more detail. They also refer to topics addressed in other books in the *Understanding Canada* series that deal with topics related to legislation, including constitutional matters, parliamentary matters, and executive matters.

What Is Legislation?

Legislation is a written form of law. It is made by bodies or persons who are authorized to make it. They cannot make it unless they have clear authority to do so.

This authority may be conferred on them by the Constitution (much of which is also legislation). In Canada, constitutional legislative authority is conferred mainly by sections 91 to 95 of the *Constitution Act, 1867*.[1] They authorize the federal Parliament and the provincial legislatures to make laws relating to various subjects. This type of legislation is generally called "primary legislation." Parliament and the legislatures are referred to as "primary legislative bodies." Although the territorial legislatures derive their legislative authority from federal legislation[2] and do not have the constitutional status of provinces,[3] the scope of their legislative powers is comparable to those of the provincial legislatures.

Most primary legislation in Canada is made either by the Parliament of Canada or by a provincial or territorial legislature.[4] It is introduced in the form of a "bill" in a legislative chamber (the Senate, the House of Commons, or a provincial or territorial assembly) and made ("enacted") through a parliamentary process resulting in a text called a "statute" or an "Act" (these terms mean the same thing). The name given to a particular piece of primary legislation usually ends with the word "Act" (for example, the *Human Rights **Act***), although the word "code" is also sometimes used (for example, the *Criminal **Code*** or the *Human Rights **Code***).

Authority to make legislation can also be conferred by primary legislation on a delegate of a primary legislative body. This type of legislation is called "delegated" or "subordinate" legislation. It is made by a vast number of different bodies and persons, basically by whomever Parliament or a legislature decides to delegate to. The principal delegates are the Governor General or Lieutenant Governor acting "in Council" (on the advice of government ministers), individual ministers, regulatory agencies (for example, the Canadian Radio-television and Telecommunication Commission (CRTC)), professional bodies (for example, the College of Physicians and Surgeons), and municipal councils (regional districts, cities, towns, villages, and townships).

What Does Legislation Do?

Legislation, like other forms of law, is intended to make it possible for people to live and work together harmoniously and productively. It does this by stating legally enforceable *rules* (requirements and prohibitions), *rights, and powers* aimed at affecting people's behaviour in ways to produce socially, economically, and environmentally beneficial results. These statements of rules, rights, and powers are generally made in grammatical sentences divided into units of text called *section*, *subsection*, *paragraph*, *subparagraph*, *clause*, and *subclause*.[5] These units are arranged hierarchically in what is known as "paragraphing" (discussed in Chapter One: What Is Drafting? under the heading "Form"). These units can also be described more generally as "provisions" because they "provide" for law.[6]

Legislation states rules, rights, and powers with a view to achieving the policy goals of those who make the legislation. There is often considerable debate about what results legislation is supposed to achieve and what legislative provisions are needed to produce these results. An important function of draft legislation is to facilitate debate about these matters and express legislative provisions as clearly as possible to achieve the results intended by those who make it.

Legislation operates in conjunction with other laws, notably common law, civil law (in Quebec), and Indigenous legal traditions. For example, the *Criminal Code* prohibition against theft uses concepts of property and ownership found in common law and civil law.[7] Theft occurs only when someone appropriates "property" that is "owned" by someone else. The *Criminal Code* does not say what property is or who owns it. These questions are answered by the common law and civil law.

Legislation often has effect through actions of officials who have power to administer or enforce it, such as the police, government employees, courts, and administrative tribunals. However, it most often has effect because people know about it and act in accordance with it. Thus, another important function of legislation is to communicate the law so that people act in accordance with it. Its written form allows it to be published and read. Most legislation in Canada is now available on internet sites such as Justice Laws Website (Canada), e-Laws (Ontario), and CanLII (Canadian Legal Information Institute).

PART ONE

Drafting and Enacting Legislation

CHAPTER ONE

What Is Drafting?

The word "drafting" has many meanings depending on its context. In relation to legislation, it has to do with writing a text to be transformed into law by a person or body with law-making authority ("law-makers"). The transformation takes place through a process culminating in a final step signifying that the process has concluded and a law has been made. For example, Acts of Parliament and the provincial and territorial legislatures are made ("enacted") through a parliamentary process ending with the assent of the Governor General, a lieutenant governor, or a commissioner. Similarly, regulations of the Governor in Council (the Governor General acting on the advice of the Cabinet) are made when the Governor General signs them.[1]

The purposes of drafting a legislative text are twofold: (1) to formulate a text that law-makers want to have the force of law in order to accomplish their policy objectives and (2) to allow the law-makers and those who are subject to the legislation to understand the law it expresses. These purposes influence how drafting is done and the role of those who draft legislative texts.

In Canada, federal, provincial, and territorial legislation is usually drafted by government lawyers, most often called "legislative" or "parliamentary" counsel. They are specialists in legislative drafting who understand what it takes to draft legislation well and have much experience doing so.[2] These specialists draft legislative texts on the basis of instructions provided by officials who develop the ideas underlying the legislation. These ideas are generally known as "legislative policy." Those who draft legislative texts and those who develop legislative policy generally work for government ministers or regulatory bodies (for example, the CRTC or public health authorities). These office-holders are, of course, also involved in developing legislative policy and providing drafting instructions in addition to approving the draft legislative texts and shepherding them through the enactment processes.[3]

Legislative texts can also be drafted by other people, including individual (outside government) parliamentarians or members of legislative assemblies, their staff and groups representing interested persons (stakeholders), or the public at large. They sometimes do so as a way of prompting governments to take legislative action.[4]

Drafting legislative texts first and foremost involves understanding the legislative policy the text is to implement and what the provisions of the text are intended to do. This aspect of drafting is discussed below and in the next chapter (How Is Legislation Drafted?).

Basic guidance on making federal legislation is provided by the *Cabinet Directive on Law-making*.[5] It delineates the key differences — in substance and in process — between primary legislation and delegated legislation (most often referred to federally as "regulations"). It also sets out the expectations of ministers in relation to the process for making federal Acts and regulations and generally orients the activities of government officials in this process. The Government of British Columbia has similar guidance documents.[6]

Once the policy is determined and understood, it must be drafted into a legislative text that will implement it effectively. This requires attention to a range of considerations and techniques that have been developed and generally accepted to produce good drafting. Many of the fundamentals of good drafting are expressed in the Legislative Drafting Conventions of the Uniform Law Conference of Canada (ULCC).[7] This organization has a long history of preparing model legislation with a view to harmonizing the laws of Canada's provinces and territories so that the same or similar laws apply in each province and territory. Its history also involves the preparation of guidance on drafting legislation, which has been formulated in the Drafting Conventions, most recently issued in 1989. The ULCC is currently reviewing and updating the Conventions.

Good drafting pays attention to many aspects of written communication and the legal system. These aspects are discussed here under the following headings:

- Language
- Legislative Policy
- Legal Effectiveness
- Form
- Provisions and Their Arrangement
- Sentence Structure
- Word Choice

Language

Legislative texts in Canada are drafted in English, French, or both languages depending on constitutional or other legal requirements governing the language in which they must be enacted.[8] Some Indigenous communities also incorporate their languages when they make laws,[9] and the legislature of Nunavut makes laws in Inuktitut as well as English and French.[10]

The Constitution requires federal Acts, as well as the Acts of Quebec, Manitoba, and New Brunswick, to be simultaneously enacted and then printed and published in both English and French.[11] This requirement also applies to delegated legislation made by the government (executive legislation) and has also been codified for federal legislation in section 13 of the *Official Languages Act*[12] and for New Brunswick legislation in section 6 of its *Official Languages Act*.[13]

Among the other provinces and the territories, there are significant differences in the degree to which they enact their laws in

English and French. Alberta, Saskatchewan, and Nova Scotia have enacted statutes in both languages on occasion,[14] but there is no legal requirement to do so.[15] Ontario takes a more rigorous approach in its *French Language Services Act*[16] and requires public bills introduced after 1 January 1991 to be introduced and enacted in both English and French. Section 4 of that Act authorizes the Lieutenant Governor in Council to require regulations to be made in French.[17]

All three territories are required to enact their legislation (both primary and delegated) in both English and French.[18] In the Northwest Territories, section 4 of the *Official Languages Act* also recognizes nine Indigenous languages in addition to English and French[19] and authorizes the translation of Acts into any of these languages. In Nunavut, the *Official Languages Act* provides that English, French, and Inuktitut are the official languages of the territory.[20] It requires legislation to be published in English and French, and that an Inuktitut version of each bill be made available when the bill is introduced in the legislature. It also authorizes the designation of an Inuit language version of an Act to be authoritative.[21]

When enacting a law in multiple languages, each version must be drafted to express the same substance while respecting the syntactical or grammatical uniqueness and expression of each language. This is particularly important when language versions have equal authenticity.

The authority of both English and French versions has been recognized under section 133 of the *Constitution Act, 1867* (dealing with federal and Quebec legislation)[22] and section 23 of the *Manitoba Act*,[23] and is explicitly affirmed in section 18 of the *Canadian Charter of Rights and Freedoms* in relation to federal and New Brunswick legislation. Provincial and territorial legislation also provides for the authority of each version. For example, *The Language Act* of Saskatchewan states that Acts and regulations may be enacted, printed, and published in English only or in English and French.[24] Section 10 of that Act provides that when legislation is enacted, printed, and published in English and French, each version is equally authoritative.[25]

Within each language, there are often specialized words and ways of saying things. Just as many other professions use specialized terminology, the legal profession uses its own terminology to express concepts that are unique to the legal system. However, just because something is expressed in legislation does not mean it has to be in specialized language. In fact, if legislation is to apply to many if not most people, it should speak to them in language they can understand. This presents a considerable challenge because of the variable capacity of people to understand written texts (literacy levels vary widely) and the complexity of the subject matter many laws deal with. Good drafting seeks a practical solution to this challenge by using ordinary language to the greatest extent possible and using specialized language only when the subject matter requires it. So, human rights codes are written in ordinary language because they apply broadly while regulations governing the operation of aircraft use some specialized language because they are used by those who operate aircraft. Good drafting considers the audience for legislative texts, but this too can be challenging when they apply to different groups with different reading abilities.[26]

Legislative Policy

A critical aspect of good drafting involves understanding the legislative policy: what the legislation is supposed to accomplish and how.

Policy formulation is a recognized discipline that is often informed by analytical frameworks designed to ensure the policy is sound. One such framework is suggested in the *Guide to Making Federal Acts and Regulations*.[27] It recognizes that legislating rules is just one of the many ways in which policy objectives can be accomplished, and that legislation is seldom if ever sufficient in itself. Examples of different "instruments" that can be used to influence behaviour involve providing information and educational programs, establishing organizations to do things, imposing charges, and providing monetary incentives. In this regard, the *Guide* suggests the following questions be considered when developing policy:

- What is the situation?
- What are the objectives in addressing the situation and what particular results are desired?
- Is there a role for the Government of Canada?
- What instruments are available to accomplish the desired results?
- What is involved in putting the instruments in place?
- What effect would the instruments have?
- How will their success be measured?
- Which (if any) instrument(s) should be chosen?

In Canada, policy making and drafting are distinct activities in the preparation of federal, provincial, and territorial legislation, although they overlap to some extent. Legislative drafters bring a sense of perspective to the formulation of legislative texts as well as a sound understanding of how legislation operates and the legal context that influences its operation. They are not experts in the subject matter of the legislation and must acquire an understanding of it that allows them to draft legislative texts to accomplish the policy objectives. They work with officials who formulate legislative policy and the drafting instructions needed to transform it into legislative text.

Legal Effectiveness

Legislative texts create rules (requirements and prohibitions), rights, and powers. Their legal effectiveness depends on whether they will be enforced in the legal system. There are many aspects of legislative drafting that determine legal effectiveness.

The most fundamental aspect is that a legislative text must clearly identify who it applies to: its legal subjects. For example, a provision simply saying doors in a nursing home must be a certain thickness cannot be enforced if it is not clear who is responsible for complying with this requirement.[28]

Legal effectiveness also depends on the clarity of legislative texts and whether they will be interpreted as intended by those who enact the legislation. Ambiguity (two or more different possible meanings) must be avoided. As for vagueness (uncertainty as to a word's range of meaning), it is inherent in the generality of laws that employ broad language to capture a wide range of circumstances. Adding detail to describe these circumstances increases the bulk of legislative texts and introduces the risk that some intended circumstances will fall between the cracks of the detail. The degree of generality (and countervailing specificity) should be carefully considered in terms of the nature and context of the legislation. For example, taxation legislation tends to be quite detailed because of how courts have tended to interpret it, requiring very clear provisions to justify collecting taxes.[29] In contrast, legislation tends toward generality in stating human rights since everyone has them and they apply to a broad range of social conduct.[30]

Yet another important aspect determining legal effectiveness is coherence with other laws. The *Constitution Act, 1867* establishes the subject matter of the legislative powers of the federal Parliament and the legislatures of the provinces.[31] If legislation does not respect this distribution of powers or is otherwise inconsistent with the Constitution, it is of no force or effect.[32] Another example of coherence has to do with delegated legislation: it must be consistent with its enabling legislation, which is the statute that gives the power to make the delegated legislation. Legislation must also be consistent with other legislation; if it is not, the inconsistency will have to be resolved through interpretation, which often involves court proceedings and may ultimately require the legislation to be amended.[33]

Form

It is usually not difficult to tell that a text is legislative. Legislation has many distinctive features that not only give it a unique look, but also help readers understand and apply it. These features result from drafting conventions that are widely shared among Canadian jurisdictions. However, there are also differences from one jurisdiction to another on matters of legislative form. It is often difficult to say one form is better than another; what is important is consistency in adhering to the form so that those who use the legislation do not have to adjust to differences from one law to another.

The most obvious distinctive feature is the division of legislative text into numbered units. The numbering makes it easier to refer to different provisions in the legislation when they are being discussed. Each sentence is generally numbered as a "section" or a "subsection" (although these units sometimes have more than one sentence). In turn, sentences can be divided into smaller units of grammatically parallel text, which can themselves be divided. These smaller units are arranged hierarchically with indentation. This formal arrangement is used to make it easier to understand long, complex sentences by exposing their grammatical structure and the relationships among their clauses and phrases.

For this arrangement to work effectively, readers must understand its underlying logic. The following example from section 6 of the *Canada Emergency Response Benefit Act* can be used to explain this logic.[34] It consists of a sentence containing 142 words. If it were presented as a single block of text, it would look like this:

> 6 (1) A worker is eligible for an income support payment if the worker, whether employed or self-employed, ceases working for reasons related to COVID-19 for at least 14 consecutive days within the four-week period in respect of which they apply for the payment; and they do not receive, in respect of the consecutive days on which they have ceased working, subject to the regulations, income from employment or self-employment, *benefits*, as defined in subsection 2(1) of the *Employment Insurance Act*, allowances, money or other benefits paid to the worker under a provincial plan because of pregnancy or in respect of the care by the worker of one or more of their new-born children or one or more children placed with them for the purpose of adoption, or any other income that is prescribed by regulation.

However, as drafted in the Act, it looks like this:

Eligibility

6 (1) A worker is eligible for an income support payment if

(a) the worker, whether employed or self-employed, ceases working for reasons related to COVID-19 for at least 14 consecutive days within the four-week period in respect of which they apply for the payment; and

(b) they do not receive, in respect of the consecutive days on which they have ceased working,

(i) subject to the regulations, income from employment or self-employment,

(ii) *benefits*, as defined in subsection 2(1) of the *Employment Insurance Act*,

(iii) allowances, money or other benefits paid to the worker under a provincial plan because of pregnancy or in respect of the care by the worker of one or more of their new-born children or one or more children placed with them for the purpose of adoption, or

(iv) any other income that is prescribed by regulation.

The arrangement makes the complex provision easier to understand by exposing its grammatical structure and the relationships among its clauses and phrases. The sentence is numbered as the first subsection of section 6—"**6 (1)**." It contains a heading—**Eligibility** (called a "section note") and is divided into "paragraphs" (called "clauses" in provincial legislation) numbered using lower case letters in parentheses: (a) and (b). Each paragraph can be read grammatically with the opening words of the subsection. They state conditions for eligibility for income support payments. Both conditions have to be met since they are joined by the conjunction "and" at the end of paragraph (a).

In turn, paragraph (b) is divided into four "subparagraphs" (called "subclauses" in provincial legislation) numbered using lower case Roman numerals in parentheses. Each of them can be read grammatically with the opening words of the paragraph and state four types of income or benefits that disentitle a worker from receiving the income support mentioned at the beginning of the subsection.

Legislative form includes headings to group related sections and section notes (like the one in the example above) to highlight their subject matter. These features help readers find the provisions they are looking for.

Typographical features are also important, including boldface to highlight particular elements (like the section note and section number in the above example).

Provisions and Their Arrangement

Legislative texts generally contain provisions arranged in the following order:

- Enacting clause [including any Preamble]
- Title
- General application and interpretation provisions, including definitions
- Purpose [these clauses may also be placed after the title]
- Substantive provisions
- Repealing, amending, transitional, and coordinating provisions
- Commencement provisions
- Schedules

Enacting Clause

An enacting clause indicates the person or body making the legislative text. The enacting clause for Acts is often set out in an Interpretation Act[35] and reads as follows for federal and provincial Acts:

> Her [His] Majesty, by and with the advice and consent of the [Senate and House of Commons of Canada/Legislative Assembly of . . .], enacts as follows:

Enacting clauses for delegated legislation also generally use the phrase "makes the annexed regulations" preceded by the name of the delegate making the legislation. For example, the enacting clause for federal regulations is:

> Her [His] Excellency the Governor General in Council, on the recommendation of the Minister of [. . .] pursuant to [*authorizing provision*] makes the annexed regulation respecting.

The enacting clause for delegated legislation may be contained in an "order" (an executive order) saying the delegated person or body makes the delegated legislation (regulation or bylaw) "annexed" (attached) to the order.

Preambles

Preambles are part of the enacting clause. They are (grammatically speaking) subordinate clauses beginning with "whereas" or "recognizing that." They state the basis for making the legislative text, but this is generally not necessary unless there is some controversy about the constitutional or other legal basis for making the legislation. An example of a preamble that — at least in part — pre-emptively addressed a constitutional controversy is Bill C-14, *An Act to amend the Criminal Code and to make related amendments to other Acts (medical assistance in dying).* That preamble contained the following statement:

> Whereas everyone has freedom of conscience and religion under section 2 of the *Canadian Charter of Rights and Freedoms*;
>
> Whereas nothing in this Act affects the guarantee of freedom of conscience and religion.[36]

Titles

Titles indicate the subject matter of the legislative text. Titles are sometimes quite lengthy and may be accompanied by "short titles" that function as labels to make it easier to refer to the legislative text.

For example, the difference is evident between the "long" title:

> An Act respecting immigration to Canada and the granting of refugee protection to persons who are displaced, persecuted or in danger

and the short title: *Immigration and Refugee Protection Act*.[37] A short title should reflect its essential subject matter. This is important for the purpose of searching for legislation on a general subject using key words.

In recent years, short titles have sometimes been used to convey messages highlighting politically attractive aspects of the legislation, such as the *Moving Ontarians More Safely Act, 2021*, which was the short title of *An Act in respect of various road safety measures*.[38]

Application Provisions

Application provisions indicate the subject matter of the legislative text or specify places where or circumstances in which it applies. For example, section 4 of the *Heritage Lighthouse Protection Act* clarifies which lighthouses that Act applies to:

> **4** This Act applies to lighthouses that are the property of Her Majesty in right of Canada.[39]

Sometimes definitions operate as application provisions when they define words that are fundamental to the application of the legislation. For example, section 2 of the *Bank Act* defines "bank."[40]

Interpretation Provisions

Interpretation provisions are rules about how the text is to be interpreted, for example, that words in the singular are to be interpreted to include the plural. This means a rule prohibiting "a person" from doing something also prohibits a group of people from doing it.

Interpretation provisions also include definitions of terms used in the legislative text. Definitions can do three things:

1) Exhaustively prescribe the meaning of terms (in which case, they use the verb "means")
2) Expand the meaning of terms (in which case, they use the verb "includes")

3) Limit the meaning of terms (in which case, they use the verb "does not include")

Most terms do not need to be defined: their ordinary meaning will apply. Definitions are used to avoid ambiguity or give a more precise meaning to terms. They may also be used to abbreviate lengthy expressions, such as names of regulatory bodies ("Canadian Radio-television and Telecommunications Commission" = "Commission")[41] or titles of documents ("Agreement between Canada, the United States of America and the United Mexican States" = "Agreement").[42]

Purpose Clauses

Purpose clauses state the general purposes of the legislative text. They can be helpful to orient legislative texts that are drafted in very general terms, particularly when they delegate broad powers. The purposes will inform the interpretation of its provisions and the exercise of the powers. Section 2 of the *Access to Information Act* is an example of a purpose provision that informs the interpretation of an Act:

> 2 (1) The purpose of this Act is to enhance the accountability and transparency of federal institutions in order to promote an open and democratic society and to enable public debate on the conduct of those institutions.[43]

Substantive Provisions

These provisions should be logically arranged. A logically arranged text usually proceeds from the general to the particular and follows the chronological sequence of events it deals with. If it deals with matters that occur in a particular order, such as court or administrative proceedings, that order should be followed.

Repealing, Amending, and Transitional Provisions

These provisions change existing legislative texts and address the effects of the changes.

A *repealing provision* removes text from the statute book so that it no longer has any legal force. The scope of a repeal can range from an entire piece of legislation (an Act, regulation, or bylaw) to particular provisions or words within an existing legislative text. *Amending provisions* are generally drafted so as to "replace" particular provisions or words with different provisions or words. Repealing and amending provisions should be drafted to identify precisely what provisions or words are repealed or amended. Each Canadian jurisdiction uses standard terminology ("amending formulae") to do this, for example:

> **x. Paragraph 2(a) of the *ABC Act* is replaced by the following:**
> **(a) weighs less than *12* tonnes;**

When a repealing or amending provision is drafted, thought must be given to two sets of further considerations.

First, will the repeal or amendment affect any other legislation? For example, if a provision changes the name of a tribunal, will its name have to be changed in any other legislation? If so, a *consequential amendment* will be needed to do this.

Second, how will a repealing or amending provision affect matters occurring before it comes into force? These questions are addressed by *transitional provisions*. For example, if someone contravenes a provision before it is repealed, can they be prosecuted for the contravention after it is repealed? Generally speaking, they can because of transitional provisions included in Interpretation Acts. For example, section 43 of the federal *Interpretation Act* says:

> **Effect of repeal**
>
> 43 Where an enactment is repealed in whole or in part, the repeal does not
>
> ...

> (d) affect any offence committed against or contravention of the provisions of the enactment so repealed, or any punishment, penalty or forfeiture incurred under the enactment so repealed, or
>
> (e) affect any investigation, legal proceeding or remedy in respect of . . . any punishment, penalty or forfeiture referred to in paragraph (d),
>
> and an investigation, legal proceeding or remedy as described in paragraph (e) may be instituted, continued or enforced, and the punishment, penalty or forfeiture may be imposed as if the enactment had not been so repealed.[44]

Transitional provisions can also deal with the effect of repeals on rights, obligations, and liabilities that have arisen under the repealed legislation.[45] For example, if legislation requires payments to be made at particular times, and payments came due before the legislation was repealed, transitional provisions in Interpretation legislation require them still to be made unless the repealing legislation provides otherwise.[46]

Transitional provisions are enacted not only in general Interpretation legislation, but also in particular Acts to deal with matters that are not clearly (or at all) addressed by the Interpretation legislation.[47] For example, section 384 of *An Act to amend the Criminal Code, the Youth Criminal Justice Act and other Acts and to make consequential amendments to other Acts* reads as follows:

> 384 Subsection 59(10) of the *Youth Criminal Justice Act* does not apply to the sentence for an offence committed before the coming into force of that subsection.[48]

Transitional provisions may also be enacted to override the general rules in Interpretation legislation that protect accrued rights.[49]

Commencement Provisions

These provisions indicate when a legislative text begins to operate as law ("commences" or "comes into force"). Although Interpretation legislation says this occurs on royal assent (for Acts) or on registration or filing (for delegated legislation), if a different commencement date is intended, legislative texts include provisions for later or (occasionally) earlier dates. These dates can be specified in the text itself, but more usually the text authorizes the government (Governor in Council or Lieutenant Governor in Council) to set the dates. The following is an example of provisions using a variety of commencement methods for various provisions:

> *Economic Action Plan Act, No. 1*, (Assented to June 26, 2013)
>
> **Coming into Force**
> **April 1, 2013**
> 103 Sections 64 to 102 are **deemed to have come into force** on April 1, 2013.
> ...
>
> **Coming into Force**
> **Order in council**
> 212 Section 211 **comes into force on a day to be fixed** by order of the Governor in Council.
>
> **Coming into Force**
> **Order in council**
> 232 Subsection 228(2) **comes into force, in accordance with subsection 114(4) of the *Canada Pension Plan*, on a day to be fixed** by order of the Governor in Council.[50]

Schedules

Schedules are sometimes attached to the end of a legislative text. They contain details to augment other provisions of the text. There are several reasons for doing this, including to avoid encumbering the text and to allow certain details to be changed more easily. An example showing the usefulness of a schedule is the one in the federal *Interpretation Act*. It lists Commonwealth countries for the purposes of the definition of "Commonwealth" in section 35 of the Act. Subsection

35(2) authorizes the Governor in Council to add or delete names of countries on the list. Another example is the schedule to the *Canada National Parks Act*, which contains detailed legal descriptions of the exact location of national parks.[51]

Incorporation by Reference

A common drafting technique involves provisions referring to another law or some document or other material, for example, standards for industry practices such as those made within the framework of the *Standards Council of Canada Act*.[52] The other law or material is incorporated into the legislation and has legal effect as if it had been reproduced word for word in the incorporating legislation.

An example of a provision incorporating another law by reference is subsection 39(2) of the *Budget Implementation Act, 1997*:

> **Collection where agreement**
>
> (2) Where a tax has been imposed by a by-law made under section 36 and an agreement entered into with the Government of British Columbia for collection of the tax, British Columbia **may collect the tax** in accordance with the agreement and may take proceedings to collect the tax **as if it were imposed under the *Tobacco Tax Act***, R.S.B.C. 1979, c. 404, as amended from time to time.[53]

An example of a provision incorporating an industry standard is in *Consumer Products Containing Lead Regulations*:

> 1 The following definitions apply in these Regulations.
>
> ***good laboratory practices*** means practices that are in accordance with the principles set out in the Organisation for Economic Co-operation and Development document entitled *OECD Principles of Good Laboratory Practice*, Number 1 of the *OECD Series on Principles of Good Laboratory Practice and Compliance Monitoring*, ENV/MC/CHEM(98)17, the English version of which is dated January 21, 1998 and the French version of which is dated March 6, 1998. (*bonnes pratiques de laboratoire*)

...

> **2 (1)** Subject to subsection (2), each accessible part of a consumer product containing lead **must not contain** more than 90 mg/kg of lead **when tested in accordance with good laboratory practices.**[54]

There are two basic types of incorporation by reference. The first involves referring to a law or other material as it existed at a particular point in time. This is known as static incorporation by reference. The preceding example from the *Consumer Products Containing Lead Regulations* illustrates this type. It incorporates documents as they existed on particular dates and requires the practices they describe to be used when testing for lead.

The other type is dynamic (also sometimes called *ambulatory* or *rolling*). It involves referring to the incorporated material as it currently exists, incorporating any changes made to it since it was originally made. The example above from the *Budget Implementation Act, 1997* illustrates this type, which is usually indicated by adding the phrase "as amended from time to time."

Incorporation by reference has two main advantages: (1) it reduces the amount of legislative text that has to be published and (2) it makes the incorporating legislation consistent with the incorporated material. Consistency with other laws, for example, laws in other provinces, territories, or countries, is often desirable to facilitate the regulation of activities that cross borders or that people carry on in different jurisdictions.

This technique also has some disadvantages. The incorporated law or material has to be found in another document. This fragmentation can make it harder to access all the material needed to understand what the legislation requires, particularly if the incorporated material is not readily accessible. There may also be linguistic barriers if the material is not available in all the legislation's official languages. And with dynamic incorporation by reference it can be difficult to verify the correct version. Dynamic incorporation by reference also raises legal concerns when used in delegated legislation since it appears to transfer (subdelegate) responsibility for making the legislation to the person or body making the incorporated material.[55] Its use is also sometimes expressly restricted by legislation governing the making of delegated legislation.[56]

Other Arrangement Considerations

Another important aspect of arrangement involves deciding what a particular piece of legislation (an Act or regulation) should deal with (its scope). Should it deal with all aspects of a policy matter, or should the matter be addressed in other pieces of legislation? For example, environmental matters were historically addressed in separate pieces of legislation, but more recently general environmental protection legislation has been enacted to deal comprehensively with these matters.[57]

Decisions about the scope of a piece of legislation affect how the matters it deals with are addressed when it is being made. The greater the scope of the legislation, the more there is for law-makers to consider. As the scope of the legislation increases, the amount of attention given to particular provisions generally decreases. This has attracted criticism to what are known as "Omnibus Bills" that enact or amend many different pieces of legislation. They most often deal with matters related to government budgets.[58] These bills are generally hundreds of pages long dealing with a host of often quite unrelated matters.[59]

Sentence Structure

Sentence structure has to do with the arrangement of words or grammatical components (clauses and phrases) in sentences. Their arrangement can lead to ambiguity about how they relate to each other (syntactic ambiguity). Good drafting is attentive to this ambiguity and seeks to avoid it. For example, the phrase "keep any device for the purpose of registering bets" is ambiguous in that "for the purpose of registering bets" may relate to "keep" or "device." The ambiguity can be avoided by saying either "keep, *for the purpose of registering bets*, any device" or "keep any device *that may be used* for the purpose of registering bets."

The usual word order in English is subject-verb-complement. The subject and verb of the main clause of a sentence express its core meaning and need to be understood before making sense of other elements of the sentence, notably subordinate clauses that qualify the main clause.

Historically, subordinate clauses stating the circumstances in which a provision applied (the "case") were stated at the beginning of a legislative sentence. However, it is difficult to understand sentences that begin with a lengthy subordinate clause. The reader has to find the main clause first to provide context for the subordinate clause. Modern drafting now places these clauses after the main clause, particularly when they are lengthy. For example, this text begins with a long subordinate clause:

> If an inspector reports to a police officer that a person has committed an indictable offence and provides details of its commission, the police officer may arrest the person.

The text is easier to understand if the main clause comes before the subordinate:

> A police officer may arrest a person if an inspector reports to the officer that the person has committed an indictable offence and provides details of its commission.

Word Choice

As noted above, legislative texts should be drafted in ordinary language. Technical language, including legal words, should be avoided unless the legislation is directed toward a technical audience or there is no other way to convey the intended meaning effectively.

Much legal language is Latin or an old form of French reflecting the historical origins of our legal system, which functioned in these languages after the Norman Conquest in 1066 and well into the fifteenth century. Bills in English were not introduced in the House of Commons until 1414.[60] Despite the transition to drafting in English, much of the Latin and law-French terminology persisted because of the meaning attributed to it. Drafters were afraid of using English words for fear of losing this meaning. Much of this fear is now unfounded and many if not most of these expressions have been replaced in modern legislative drafting in Canada. For example, the Latin expression, "*ex parte*" has been replaced by "without notice" in the Ontario *Rules of Civil Procedure*.[61] Some words conveying uniquely legal ideas continue to be used because they have no modern equivalent (for example, *mandamus*, meaning a type of order a court can make when it reviews the actions of government) or have themselves come into popular usage (for example, "mortgage").

One of the basic principles of legislative drafting is to avoid repetition. Saying the same thing twice not only makes more work for readers, it also opens the door to arguments that different things are intended. However, this principle was often violated in the past in an effort to make legislation more understandable by using English words in addition to Latin and law French. For example, wills were drafted to say the testator "gives, devises and bequeaths" their estate according to the terms of the will. Each of these words means the same thing. They differ in their linguistic origin: *give* is modern English, *devise* is French, and *bequeath* is Old English. Similarly, in the expression "null and void," *null* is Latin and *void* is French. Today, there is little need for these doublets and triplets. A single word ("give" or "void") will do.

CHAPTER TWO

How Is Legislation Drafted?

Drafters and Drafting Offices

The drafting processes discussed in this chapter are offered as detailed examples of how federal legislation is drafted. Drafting processes in provinces, territories, municipalities, and other legislative bodies vary, but they generally follow the main steps outlined here.

Although law-makers could themselves draft legislation, most of this highly specialized work is done by lawyers called "legislative" or "parliamentary" counsel. These titles are used interchangeably in various jurisdictions, but this book refers to them generally as legislative counsel. They are lawyers with specialized training who work to create clear, unambiguous, and enforceable statements of legal rules, rights, and powers (see Chapter One: What Is Drafting?). Every step of the drafting process requires legal analysis and decisions on how best to develop and express a legal provision. This requires extensive knowledge of constitutional law in order to respect federal, provincial, and territorial jurisdictional limits, as well as other generally applicable legislation relating to such matters as human rights, access to information, privacy, official languages, and legislative processes and interpretation.

Legislative counsel must also carefully analyze how legislative proposals would fit into or align with any existing legislation in the relevant area of law. Conflicts or inconsistency in legislation must be avoided since they create doubts about the meaning of legislation, which can in turn lead to disputes that have to be resolved by courts and tribunals.

Legislative counsel generally work in drafting offices affiliated with either the government or with a legislative body such as the Senate, the House of Commons, or a provincial or territorial legislative assembly.

Drafting offices may also include legislative revisors and jurilinguists, who are linguistic experts. They review draft legislation for grammar, terminology, and coherence, as well as to ensure it follows established drafting standards and format (see Chapter One: What Is Drafting?). In jurisdictions where legislation is made in more than one language, the review includes ensuring the language versions of the legislation say the same thing (see Chapter One: What Is Drafting? — Language). In some offices, translators prepare one of the language versions of the draft legislative text.

It is essential that legislative counsel understand the instructions and legislative policy underlying a legislative initiative. This understanding is key to designing the legislation required to achieve the goals described in the policy. It is also key to determining how the legislation may fit into existing legislation, for example, whether it should be a new stand-alone act or regulation or should instead be integrated into existing legislation by amending it. Legislative provisions must be drafted to ensure that all the elements needed to implement the underlying policy are identified and considered so that the intended effect can be achieved.

Government Drafting Offices

Historically, government legislation at the federal level was drafted by the relevant department responsible for the legislation.[1] Since 1948, primary legislation (government bills) has been centrally drafted by legislative counsel in the Legislation Section of the Department of Justice. This results from a Cabinet requirement of Cabinet approval for drafting to begin.

There is considerable variation in the drafting of government legislation in the provinces and territories.[2] In some, bills are drafted by legislative counsel in a government department such as a ministry of justice or the attorney general.[3] In Quebec, bills are drafted in the department that is responsible for them, subject to review by the Ministère du Conseil exécutif. In other provinces and territories, primary legislation is drafted by a legislative counsel office associated with the legislative assembly.[4] These offices may also draft delegated legislation,[5] or it may be drafted in the particular government departments that sponsor it.

Most statutes result from bills introduced by government ministers on behalf of the government as a whole with the approval of other ministers (the Cabinet). Government-wide processes are used to coordinate and set priorities among proposals for bills from different departments; the result forms the legislative program for the government.[6] At the federal level, a Cabinet directive requires ministers to prepare a Memorandum to Cabinet (MC) that describes and justifies their legislative proposals and to present the MC to Cabinet for consideration.[7]

The drafting of delegated legislation (regulations) is centralized federally and in many provinces and territories. The centralization occurred federally with the enactment of the *Statutory Instruments Act* in 1970. It requires all draft regulations to be reviewed by the Clerk of the Privy Council on the advice of the deputy minister of justice.[8] This resulted in the establishment of units (Regulations Sections) within the Department of Justice that not only review draft regulations but in most cases draft them as well. There are also certain departments that generate a high volume of regulatory work (for example, Health Canada and Transport Canada). These are served by units that develop particular expertise in the legal and legislative context that applies to those departments and draft exclusively for them.

Parliamentary Drafting Offices

Legislators who are not Cabinet ministers can also introduce bills in the legislative chambers in which they sit. At the federal level senators and members of the House of Commons who are not in the Cabinet may introduce bills called "public bills" in the Senate and "private members' bills" in the House of Commons. The legislative policy, drafting instructions, and objectives of these bills tend to be much less comprehensive than for government bills since non-government members do not have access to governmental policy and legal resources to develop legislative initiatives. Their bills are prepared by legislative counsel in either the Senate or the House of Commons Law Clerk's Office. At the provincial or territorial level, individual members of those assemblies may also propose bills, which are prepared by drafting offices attached to the assemblies. In some provincial and territorial assemblies, legislative counsel in the government draft for both government and opposition members.[9] Drafting offices must avoid conflicts of interest that may otherwise arise in such circumstances by adjusting their work processes accordingly, notably by maintaining strict confidentiality.

Who Else Is Involved in Drafting?

Drafters and drafting offices work closely with many others outside their offices to prepare draft legislation. Most obviously, legislators and their staff are involved as the main drivers and recipients of draft legislation.

For government legislation, this means Cabinet ministers and the offices that support them, including Cabinet offices such as the Privy Council Office and the Treasury Board Secretariat (federal government), the Executive Council Office (Ontario), and the Ministère du Conseil exécutif (Quebec). These offices support the Cabinet and coordinate its legislative activities, including the drafting of legislation.

Another important group involved in government legislative drafting consists of officials in the various government departments or ministries who are responsible for developing and implementing government policy. They provide detailed support in terms of analyzing how policies should be implemented, including whether legislation is required. They also develop the instructions that legislative counsel require to draft legislation (see below: Drafting Primary Legislation — Drafting Instructions).

A third important group providing support for government legislative drafting are legal advisers, including those who provide legal support to particular departments or ministries as well as specialists who provide advisory services in particular fields of law such as constitutional and administrative law.

Finally, the offices of legislative counsel in the Senate and the House of Commons are supported by the Library of Parliament, which provides extensive research to senators and members of Parliament who may be considering particular legislative initiatives.

Drafting Process

Drafting legislation is a complex process. Legislation creates rules, rights, and powers that have wide-reaching and profound effects. Draft legislation may cover the full range of matters falling within the jurisdiction of the relevant law-making body. For this reason, essential checks and balances have been built into the process of making legislation. These ensure that the law-making body has looked at all aspects of the subject area of the legislation and determined that legislation is necessary. This threshold question is of the utmost importance when considering legislative measures. Most policy objectives cannot be achieved by legislation alone. Government objectives are often more effectively pursued by non-legislative measures such as public education, agreements, and guidelines or, more generally, programs for providing services, benefits, or increasing the capacity of people or organizations to advance policy objectives.[10]

Legislative drafting involves a series of activities:

- Drafting instructions (understanding and refining them with instructing officials)
- Designing the legislative structure and organizing the text
- Drafting (writing) the text in the required format
- Reviewing and refining the text
- Finalizing it

While these activities vary among Canadian drafting offices, most share the same fundamental elements. This chapter describes these phases in terms of the federal process, first in relation to primary legislation and then in relation to delegated legislation. Although this description focuses on the federal process, it has much in common with processes in the provinces and territories. The differences are largely ones of scale: more actors are involved at the federal level and some processes are more elaborate.

One key difference, which arises in the case of multilingual legislation, is whether both language versions are drafted simultaneously (co-drafting), or whether one language version is translated from the other. In the case of New Brunswick and federal government drafting offices, legislation is co-drafted by a team of two legislative counsel, one working on the French version, the other on the English version (see below, Drafting Bilingual and Bijural Legislation). In other offices, legislation is drafted in one language and translated into the other.

Drafting Primary Legislation

Primary legislation is drafted in the form of a "bill" to be introduced in a legislative chamber (the Senate, the House of Commons, or a legislative assembly). The main phases for drafting primary legislation are set out below under the following headings:

- Drafting Instructions
- Drafting Bills

- Review and Refinement
- Approval for Introduction

Drafting Instructions

GOVERNMENT BILLS (FEDERAL)

Government bills are generally drafted only after the Cabinet has given its approval for them to be drafted. Prior approval, based on a Memorandum to Cabinet (MC), gives clear authority and direction for drafting. The MC sets out the issue, objectives, and scope of the proposed bill, and provides instructions on how it is to be drafted. In recent years, the Leader of the Government in the House of Commons has exercised authority delegated from the Cabinet to approve bill-drafting before MC approval where time constraints exist.

The steps generally involved in approving and implementing drafting instructions for federal government bills are:

1. An MC is prepared by policy officials in the department of the responsible minister and with their legal advisers; it sets out the issues to be addressed, as well as the objectives and scope of the proposed bill and any regulations to be authorized under it. Drafting instructions are annexed to the MC.
2. The MC is reviewed by central departments (Privy Council Office, Finance, and Treasury Board Secretariat) and discussed at meetings with other departments.
3. The MC is considered by a Cabinet committee and, if approved, the Privy Council Office issues a Cabinet Committee Report (CR), which is then considered by the full Cabinet. If the CR is ratified, the Privy Council Office issues a Record of Decision (RD). Both the CR and the RD are based on the recommendations and drafting instructions contained in the original MC.
4. The RD is sent to the Legislation Section of the Department of Justice with instructions to draft the proposed bill.
5. The Deputy Chief Legislative Counsel assigns the bill to a team (or teams in the case of very large bills) of two legislative

counsel: one to draft the French version, the other to draft the English version.

6. Each assigned counsel reviews the instructions and studies the legal and legislative issues. The two legislative counsel discuss questions and determine measures to achieve the objective, as well as how the proposed text would fit into or with any existing legislation.
7. The legislative counsel share their questions and suggestions with the departmental policy official and their legal advisers, work together on any outstanding legal or legislative issues, and may flag policy issues of a technical nature relating to matters such as when the new legislation should come into force.

PARLIAMENTARY (SENATORS' OR PRIVATE MEMBERS') BILLS

The steps generally involved in developing and implementing instructions to draft bills for parliamentarians (senators and members of the House of Commons) are:

1A. Parliamentarians consider ideas for bills based on issues of interest, particularly to their constituents. They and their staff may develop an idea to varying degrees.

2A. Parliamentarians may seek non-legal advice and guidance from the Library of Parliament on the historical or social context of the idea, whether it has been the subject of legislation before, and to flag any possible issues (for example, if the proposal would encroach on an area of provincial jurisdiction).

3A. Parliamentarians may discuss their idea with colleagues in their party's caucus or choose not to do so.

4A. The proposal is sent to legislative counsel in the Law Clerk's Office.

5A. A file is assigned to a legislative counsel to draft the bill in the language of the sponsoring parliamentarian's choice.

6A. The legislative counsel reviews the instructions and identifies any legal or legislative issues, considers measures to achieve the objective, and ensures that it fits its legislative context. Review includes, as applicable, discussions about whether the bill is inconsistent with the purposes and provisions of the *Canadian Bill of Rights*[11] and the *Canadian Charter of Rights and Freedoms*,[12] and whether there are other constitutional issues, such as encroaching on provincial jurisdiction.

7A. The legislative counsel shares questions with the parliamentarian and their staff, outlining any issues and proposed solutions or changes.

Drafting Bills

GOVERNMENT BILLS (FEDERAL)

The steps generally involved in drafting federal government bills are:

8. The assigned legislative counsel are responsible for preparing the draft bill. Drafting may be done in a meeting (drafting) room in which the legislative counsel work with departmental policy experts and departmental legal counsel to refine the legislative text. These rooms may be equipped with computers to facilitate simultaneous drafting in both languages (co-drafting), with additional seating and display screens so that department officials and their legal advisers can see the text, make comments, and respond to suggestions as drafting proceeds.[13]
9. The legislation is drafted clearly in a way that follows established drafting standards. The text is presented in a standardized format for federal legislation in Canada.[14] This format relies on detailed structural units to organize the legislative text and uses elements that make the text as accessible as possible to read and understand (see Chapter One: What Is Drafting?).
10. In some jurisdictions, legislative counsel draft using computer applications that encode the text in structural units to format its eventual publication.

PARLIAMENTARY (SENATORS' OR PRIVATE MEMBERS') BILLS

The steps generally involved in drafting these bills are:

8A. The legislative counsel prepares a draft of the bill in the language of the instructing parliamentarian.
9A. (As in 9 above).
10A. (As in 10 above).

Review and Refinement

GOVERNMENT BILLS (FEDERAL)

The steps generally involved for reviewing and refining these bills are:

11. Once a viable draft exists, each legislative counsel submits their draft to legislative revisors (also often referred to as editors) who edit it for grammar, terminology, coherence, and conformity with established drafting standards and format; if the bill amends existing legislation, they also review the arrangement, terminology, and phrasing of the draft text so that it fits within the existing legislative context. Jurilinguists and bijuralists conduct additional revision to ensure both language versions say the same thing and can apply in relation to both common and civil law.[15]
12. Legislative counsel closely consider the comments and suggestions of the revisors, jurilinguists, and bijuralists, discussing any appropriate changes.
13. Once legislative counsel are satisfied with the draft, they share it with the departmental officials and their legal counsel for comment or approval. Numerous drafts may be shared for review and eventual approval by the senior officials and ministers. Legislative revisors, jurilinguists, and bijuralists review any further drafts as needed.

PARLIAMENTARY (SENATORS' OR PRIVATE MEMBERS') BILLS

The steps generally involved for reviewing and refining these bills are:

11A. Once a viable draft exists in one language, the legislative counsel submits it to jurilinguists who conduct a preliminary review; the draft is then sent to legislative translators who prepare the other language version. The jurilinguists then review both versions performing the editorial and revision functions noted above in 11.

12A. The legislative counsel closely considers the comments and suggestions of the jurilinguists and translators, discussing any appropriate changes. A peer review may also be conducted by sharing the draft bill with other legislative counsel for comment.

13A. (As in 13 above, but with the parliamentarian or their staff).

Approval for Introduction

GOVERNMENT BILLS (FEDERAL)

The steps generally involved for approving these bills for introduction are:

14. The final text is reviewed by the sponsoring minister and submitted to the Leader of the Government in the House of Commons for approval.
15. The Leader of the Government in the House of Commons reviews the bill to ensure it is consistent with relevant Cabinet decisions and decides whether to seek delegated authority from the Cabinet to approve it for introduction.
16. The legislative counsel in the Department of Justice, on behalf of the minister of justice, examine the bill to ascertain whether it is inconsistent with the purposes and provisions of the *Canadian Bill of Rights* and the *Canadian Charter of Rights and Freedoms* and reports any ascertained inconsistency to the House of Commons.[16]
17. Once approved for introduction, the final print version of the proposed bill is sent to the Journals Branch of the House of Commons or, in the case of the Senate, to Chamber Operations and Procedure in print and electronic format to be put on notice for subsequent introduction.

PARLIAMENTARY (SENATORS' OR PRIVATE MEMBERS') BILLS

The steps generally involved for approving these bills for introduction are:

14A. The final text is reviewed by the sponsoring parliamentarian and may be shared with their party's caucus, colleagues, or interested stakeholders if the parliamentarian wishes.

15A. The caucus may review the bill to determine its consistency with its party's platform and decide whether to support the bill; however, approval is not necessary for introduction. Colleagues or stakeholders may review the bill to determine whether to support it.

16A. A final approved version of the bill is sent by the parliamentarian to the Journals Branch of the House of Commons or, in the case of the Senate, to Chamber Operations and Procedure, in print and electronic format to be put on notice for subsequent introduction.

17A. If the bill is introduced and added to the Order of Precedence,[17] a further review is conducted by the Subcommittee on Private Members' Business at the House of Commons. It may determine that the bill is non-votable and, if so, it will not be allowed to proceed further.

Confidentiality

Draft bills and supporting documents are subject to one or more types of confidentiality, often referred to as "privilege." This means they are protected and cannot be shared unless the person who holds the privilege (the Cabinet or sponsoring parliamentarian) authorizes their release. This constraint affects the drafting process by putting strict limitations on sharing certain documents.

Draft bills and supporting documents that contain legal advice are protected by solicitor-client privilege. If they form the basis for Cabinet decision-making or the discussions and deliberations of Cabinet ministers, they are also Cabinet confidences and so protected from unauthorized disclosure on that basis. When notice is given for introduction of a bill, it is subject to parliamentary privilege, which means it must not be distributed elsewhere before being introduced. The version of the bill that is actually introduced in Parliament is not subject to these privileges. The privileges apply only to the previous draft versions.

Drafting Delegated Legislation

Delegated legislation is made under authority delegated by Parliament or a provincial or territorial legislature in a statute (an "enabling Act"). In terms of volume, most legislation is delegated legislation. There are three principal types:

- One is made by the executive branch of government. It consists of what are called regulations or executive legislation. It is made under authority to make laws on certain aspects in a legislative scheme, which are described to varying degrees in the enabling Act. Federal regulations are most often made by the Governor in Council, which is composed of the Governor General acting on the advice of the Cabinet (which is currently provided by a Cabinet committee — the Treasury Board). Provincial and territorial regulations are made by comparable bodies (the Lieutenant Governor in Council or the Commissioner in Council). Authority to make regulations may also be delegated to individual ministers or regulatory bodies such as the CRTC.
- A second type is made by courts and tribunals. This type consists of what are generally called rules of procedure.
- The third type is made by municipal bodies, such as city or town councils and transit authorities. This type consists of what are generally called bylaws.

At the federal level in Canada, most executive legislation is drafted by legislative counsel in the Department of Justice based on instructions from officials in government departments or other bodies that have authority to make the legislation. Executive legislation is usually called a **regulation**, but it can also be called an **order**, **rule**, or **bylaw**.[18]

Many of the drafting steps relating to federal primary legislation also apply in preparing federal regulations. They are prepared on the basis of policy instructions approved by the responsible minister or other regulation-making body in collaboration with policy experts and legal advisers from the responsible department or body. They are co-drafted by pairs of legislative counsel and follow the same pattern of review by legislative revisors, jurilinguists, and bijuralists. There are, however, certain significant differences between drafting delegated legislation and primary legislation. One difference is the focus that must be placed on ensuring that the text of the delegated legislation is aligned with, and stays within the boundaries of, the enabling Act. Failure to ensure this could mean that portions of a regulation may be invalid because they are inconsistent with, or outside the authority (*ultra vires*) of, the enabling Act. Another significant difference is that most regulations made by the Governor in Council or a minister are published in draft form before they are made (a step referred to as pre-publication). Members of the public are invited to send comments on the draft regulations to the department responsible for them. This may result in changes to the version of the regulation that is submitted for final approval.

Some provinces and territories have centralized drafting arrangements like those of the federal government.[19] However, in others, regulations are drafted in the department responsible for them.[20] Drafting delegated legislation also entails similar processes for the approval of policy instructions, review, and final approval by ministers.

Drafting Bilingual and Bijural Legislation

The Constitution requires federal legislation and the legislation of Quebec, Manitoba, and New Brunswick to be made in both English and French.[21] Federal legislation also has to apply across the country, both in Quebec, which has a civil law system of private law (governing property and civil rights as between private individuals and corporations), and the other provinces and territories, which have a common law system of private law. In other words, federal laws must be drafted to speak to both English-speakers and French-speakers. In addition, when federal legislation involves matters of property and civil rights, the legislation must be drafted to reflect both civil law and common law concepts.

Bilingual Legislation

Federal legislation, both primary and delegated, is drafted to reflect Canada's bilingual and bijural nature. To achieve this, federal government legislation is **co-drafted** by two legislative counsel: one is responsible for the French version and one is responsible for the English version. Drafting may be done in a meeting (drafting) room equipped with computers to facilitate simultaneous drafting in both languages, in the presence of department officials and their legal advisers who can see the text, make comments, and respond to suggestions as drafting proceeds in both languages.

In co-drafting, neither version is a translation of the other. "The objective is to produce two original and authentic versions through the close and constant cooperation of the two drafters."[22] Each legislative counsel prepares a draft of the bill, ensuring the text achieves its legislative objective in a way that respects the unique character of each language (structure, syntax, and terminology).

In addition to legislative revisors, linguistic experts with extensive knowledge of legislative language in both English and French (referred to as "jurilinguists") review the draft text in each language for equivalence with the other language version.

Co-drafting is also practised in New Brunswick, but most other jurisdictions in Canada that enact bilingual legislation do so by drafting the text in one language and having it translated into the other. Translators may be brought into the drafting process at different points, and not necessarily at the end.[23] Employing either technique has the benefit of clarifying the expression of the law in both languages by adding necessary precision and nuance.

Bijural Legislation

Legislation and the processes for making it form a distinct part of our legal system in Canada. As such, legislation and the legislative processes are not based on common law or civil law. However, because of its history of colonization by France and Great Britain, two legal traditions coexist in Canadian private law: the civil law and the common law. The law governing relationships between private individuals and corporations is based on either the English common law or (in Quebec) civil law. As a result, where federal legislation touches on property and civil rights, it must refer to both civil law and common law concepts so that the application of the law is clear all across Canada.

The bijural character of federal legislation is recognized in section 8.1 of the federal *Interpretation Act*, which states:

> 8.1 Both the common law and the civil law are equally authoritative and recognized sources of the law of property and civil rights in Canada and, unless otherwise provided by law, if in interpreting an enactment it is necessary to refer to a province's rules, principles or concepts forming part of the law of property and civil rights, reference must be made to the rules, principles and concepts in force in the province at the time the enactment is being applied.[24]

Federal legislation is accordingly reviewed by bijuralists (experts in comparative law), who review both versions to identify potential problems in terminology or related to the application of a provision when federal legislation incorporates the private law of property and civil rights in the provinces or territories.

From a drafting perspective, reflecting the bijural dimension of the law of property and civil rights means that such legislation will include both common law terms and civil law terms (specific terms) or terms that apply in both systems (generic terms). For example, the civil law concept of a "hypothec" is similar to a "mortgage" in common law and the result of applying each is substantially the same. To be certain legislation referring to a "hypothec" or a "mortgage" will apply across the country, both terms must be used. See, for example, the definition of "purchaser" in section 48 of the *Canada Business Corporations Act*:

> **Purchaser** means a person who takes an interest or right in a security by sale, mortgage, hypothec, pledge, issue, reissue, gift or any other voluntary transaction.[25]

An example of generic terminology is the use of "legal counsel" and "*conseiller juridique*." These terms have equivalent meaning in both the common law and civil law.[26]

CHAPTER THREE

How Is Draft Legislation Turned Into Law?

Primary Legislation

After a bill has been drafted, it passes through a series of stages in Parliament or, in the case of the provinces or territories, their legislatures.

Parliament consists of three components: the king and two legislative chambers or Houses (the Senate and the House of Commons). Each provincial and territorial legislature consists of two components: the lieutenant governors (or the commissioners in the territories) and a chamber or House called a legislative assembly (or the National Assembly in Quebec).

At the federal level, bills can be introduced in either the Senate or the House of Commons, with the exception of bills dealing with the imposition of taxes or spending public money, which must be introduced in the House of Commons first.[1]

Once introduced in a House, the bill goes through several stages in which it can be studied, debated, and adopted in that House. It is then introduced in the other House, where it can again be studied, debated, and adopted.

The main stages in each House are:

- Introduction and First Reading
- Second Reading
- Committee Study
- Report Stage
- Third Reading
- Royal Assent

The stages a bill must go through provide opportunities for parliamentarians (both government and opposition) to understand and examine a bill, voice their opinions on its merits, consider its context and any related issues, justify or critically analyze the bill, and change or reshape it. The stages of the legislative process are rooted in the history of the British parliamentary tradition. Many of these stages still reflect formalities that have existed since the time when bills were labouriously transcribed onto parchment and read out loud in their entirety for the consideration and approval of the sovereign. The federal legislative process is largely governed by the Rules of the Senate and the Standing Orders of the House of Commons.[2] Provincial and territorial assemblies have comparable rules of procedure.[3] Opportunities to amend a bill arise at two stages in the legislative process: when it is studied by a committee and at report stage.

Introduction and First Reading

A bill may be introduced only after notice of the intention to introduce it has been given to the House or legislative assembly in which it is to be introduced. This notice informs the House or legislative assembly that a bill about a certain subject may be introduced. The notice does not include the bill itself, just limited information such as the title and the name of the sponsoring member. Introduction of a bill requires the sponsoring member to indicate to the clerk of the House or assembly that they wish to proceed with the bill. It is then included in the legislative business of the day. The bill will be assigned a number, which in the federal Parliament distinguishes where the bill originates (Senate or House of Commons), and whether the bill is a government bill, private members' bill, or Senate public bill.

Leave to introduce a bill is granted automatically and the bill is ready to be "read" a first time. In fact, any actual reading of the bill at first reading has been dispensed with since the early 1600s. In the federal context, the Speaker of the House proposes a motion "That this bill be now read a first time and be printed" and the motion is automatically carried. First reading of a bill does not equate to any support on the part of the House except that it be made publicly available, both in print and digitally.[4]

Second Reading

When a bill makes its way to second reading, a vote is taken on whether to debate it and refer it subsequently to a specified committee for study. Second reading provides the first opportunity for a debate on the bill. This debate is not about its specific provisions, but rather relates to its principle and scope. To start debate, the sponsoring member makes a motion "That Bill (*number and title)* be now read a second time and referred to the (*name of committee*)." What follows is a series of speeches from the sponsoring member and other members of the House who debate the principle of the bill. Debate on a bill usually takes place over several days during the scheduled time in the House's agenda. After debate is concluded, the bill is referred to a committee for closer, detailed examination. [5]

Committee Study

Committee study provides an opportunity to examine a bill and its provisions closely.[6] To some extent, committees are the workhorses of the Houses that constitute them. Their responsibility is to consider the bill in detail. This is as much a measure of efficiency as anything else because it effectively allocates legislative proposals to the appropriate committee, which has the particular expertise or understanding of the matters of the bills referred to them.

Committees often establish and maintain specializations in certain areas of law and are re-constituted at the beginning of each Parliament to continue addressing their particular area of focus. (For example, in the House of Commons, the Standing Committee on Industry and Technology focuses on the activities of Industry Canada and issues related to industry, technology, scientific research, telecommunications, trade, investment, and small business. The Standing Committee on Justice and Human Rights focuses on the bills, policies, programs, and spending of the Department of Justice, as well as the Human Rights Commission and other federal entities involved in the administration of justice.) The assigned committee studies the bill, hears from witnesses invited by the committee chair on request of each party, and closely examines the bill's provisions.

The detailed examination of the bill's provisions is referred to as the clause-by-clause study. During that phase, each provision ("clause") of the bill is considered individually. Amendments to each clause may be proposed by the member sponsoring the bill or any parliamentarians who sit on the committee. Procedural rules limit the type of amendments that may be proposed and voted on at committee.[7] These limits mainly depend on whether the amendments fall within the principle and scope of the bill at second reading. The chair of the committee during its study decides whether amendments are admissible.

Amendments are drafted either by legislative counsel working for the government (in the case of government-sponsored amendments) or by legislative counsel in the relevant parliamentary chamber (in the case of amendments proposed by other parliamentarians). In some provincial and territorial assemblies, such as Ontario, legislative counsel in the government draft for both government and opposition members. These drafting offices must avoid any conflicts of interest that may otherwise arise in such circumstances.

Report Stage

Following the committee stage, a bill is reported back to the House with or without amendments. Additional amendments may also be considered by the House at report stage if there is no opportunity to bring them at the committee stage. Again, procedural rules apply to assist the Speaker of the House in determining which amendments may be considered at report stage and voted on at third reading.[8]

Drafting Amendments

The drafting process for preparing amendments is very similar to the process for drafting the bill and basically follows steps two to fourteen set out in Chapter 2 (How Is Legislation Drafted?; see Drafting Process — Primary Legislation). However, the entire process, from developing instructions for an amendment to drafting it, occurs at a much more accelerated pace. This is largely driven by the legislative timetable of either House, which can mean that there may be very little time between the activities at each stage of the legislative process. For example, during the committee's study of a bill there may be less than forty-eight hours between hearing from witnesses and voting on individual clauses of the bill.

Drafting amendments, particularly at committee stage, is the best opportunity for parliamentarians to influence the final text of a bill in a way that may reflect party, public, or stakeholder positions on a matter. Parliamentarians may be looking for ways to amend the bill, and the nature of specific changes often takes shape as witnesses are heard at committee and during the clause-by-clause examination of a bill. Government-sponsored amendments may also be prepared, whether to respond to academic or stakeholder input or public reaction to the bill. In searching for a way to amend a bill, opposition and backbench parliamentarians often explore a range of possible amendments before selecting those that would be the most appropriate and effective ways to meet their particular objectives.

Preparing amendments in this context is often quite labour intensive given the shifting possibilities and tight timeframe, as well as the need to ensure the amendment is legally defensible and fits with the other provisions of the bill in terminology, purpose, and scope. These challenges can result in significant work for legislative counsel, particularly if a bill generates widespread public and stakeholder interest. For example, during clause-by-clause examination in the House of Commons of Bill C-14 —*An Act to Amend the Criminal Code and to make related amendments to other Acts (medical assistance in dying)*[9] approximately eighty amendments were tabled at committee.[10] Sixteen were adopted at committee and then formed part of the bill as reported back to the House following committee stage. There followed ten proposed amendments at report stage, none of which was adopted. Subsequent consideration of the bill in the Senate generated a significant number of proposed amendments, as well as several messages between the Houses, with the House accepting some of the Senate amendments and modifying or rejecting others before the text of the bill was agreed to by both Houses and royal assent was conferred.[11]

Third Reading

Following debate at report stage, the House considers the bill at third reading and votes on any amendments that may have been moved at report stage. If the bill is adopted at third reading, it has been passed by the House and is sent to the other House, where essentially the same steps are followed.

Messages Between the Houses

On occasion, the two federal Houses of Parliament do not initially agree on the legislative text of the bill. In such cases, a message is sent to the other House indicating the provisions it agrees with, disagrees with, or seeks to amend. The message may include other observations or recommendations about the bill. The message is considered by the House and the government determines its position on the proposed amendments. Parliamentarians then vote on the final response to the other House and a message is sent back in response. This process can continue, with messages being sent back and forth between the Senate and the House of Commons, until both Houses agree on the legislation. Although in theory the exchange of messages between the two Houses is not limited in time or number, agreement is usually reached within a relatively short time. If one House votes to approve a bill passed by the other House without amendment, the bill is ready to be sent to the Governor General for royal assent.

Royal Assent

Once a bill has been passed in the same form by both Houses, it is sent to the Governor General for royal assent. Bills passed by a provincial or territorial legislative assembly are sent to the lieutenant governor or commissioner for royal assent. A bill that has received royal assent has been made ("enacted") and becomes an Act of Parliament (also known as a Statute of Canada) or an Act of the province or territory.

Most royal assents of the Governor General are given in the form of a written declaration signed by the Governor General. But at least once each session of Parliament, a traditional royal assent ceremony is conducted in which the business of the Senate is suspended and the Governor General attends in the Senate Chamber to give royal assent in the presence of senators as well as members of the House of Commons, who are formally summoned "to attend immediately in the Senate Chamber" and are escorted by the sergeant-at-arms of the Senate in a procession from the House of Commons to the Senate Chamber. Once all are assembled in the Senate, the Governor General signifies assent to the bills by a nod of the head, and the members of the House of Commons leave, followed by the Governor General.[12]

Not all bills introduced in the Senate, the House of Commons, or a Legislative Assembly are enacted. When Parliament or the

Legislature is dissolved for an election, any bills left unfinished (as well as all its other business) are terminated (referred to as "dying on the order paper").

Publication

In addition to drafting legislation, most drafting offices also publish it. In the federal context, most bills are printed and made available publicly within a few hours after introduction and first reading.[13] This allows interested people to read each bill as it is introduced, as well as any amended versions of the bill as it progresses through the legislative process, and then the final version once it becomes law. Each version of federal bills is available online through the parliamentary LegisInfo website.[14] Publication is done digitally and in print. Provincial and territorial assemblies also publish their own bills online.

Publication is an exercise in precision and timeliness. There is no margin for error, and the texts need to be published as soon as possible so they are available to all interested persons both during the enactment process and once they become law. The publication process is supported by information technology (IT) technicians who work closely with the legislative counsel and the supporting revision team. The *Canada Gazette* publishes federal statutes and regulations.[15] In addition, the Department of Justice maintains the Justice Laws Website, which is the online source of the official consolidated Acts and regulations of Canada.[16] Provincial and territorial governments maintain sites to provide access to their published laws.[17]

Delegated Legislation

Executive Legislation (Regulations)

Canadian regulatory practices and policies generally emphasize the importance of consultation and transparency in making regulations given their significance and impact. This allows those affected by proposed regulations to comment on and understand their potential impact.[18]

The federal regulatory process is designed to require most draft regulations (those made by the Governor in Council or a minister) to be published before they are made into law. The *Canada Gazette* publishes the proposed version of such regulations. Many provincial policies include this pre-publishing step as well,[19] particularly in the case of proposed regulations that have an impact on business. For example, Ontario has a policy-based pre-publication step that applies only to regulations that have an impact on business.[20] In contrast, British Columbia's Regulatory Reform Policy applies to statutes, regulations, and associated policies and forms that require people or businesses to "complete an action" to comply with legislation or to access government services.[21] Quebec has taken the additional step of codifying its regulatory regime, which includes a pre-publication requirement, in a statute.[22]

Once drafted, executive legislation generally follows a process for its approval, publication, and (occasionally) parliamentary review. These processes are established by a combination of statutory and policy requirements.

The process for most federal regulations is set out in the *Cabinet Directive on Regulation*.[23] It includes the following steps:

1. **Pre-publishing.** This step applies as a matter of policy to regulations made by the Governor in Council or a minister. A proposed regulation is to be pre-published in *Canada Gazette* Part I. This provides formal notice of the proposed regulation and sets a time period during which the public may comment. It is accompanied by a detailed impact statement that explains the basic ideas in the proposed regulation and describes the potential positive and negative impacts it would have on people, businesses, and government. The *Cabinet Directive on Regulation* specifies the detailed analysis that must accompany the proposed regulation and its impacts, including health, safety, Indigenous, environmental, financial, and employment impacts. Changes that flow

from comments after pre-publication may be made to the text of the regulation.

2. **Reporting.** The Clerk of the Privy Council, in consultation with the Minister of Justice, must, under section 3 of the *Statutory Instruments Act*, examine proposed regulations to ensure that:
   (a) they are authorized by the statute under which they are made,
   (b) they do not constitute an unusual or unexpected use of the regulation making power,
   (c) they do not trespass unduly on rights and freedoms and are not inconsistent with the *Charter of Rights and Freedoms* or the *Canadian Bill of Rights*, and
   (d) the form and drafting of the regulations meet established standards.[24]

   The clerk must indicate to the regulation-making authority any of these matters to which, in the opinion of the deputy minister of justice, based on the examination, the attention of the regulation-making authority should be drawn.[25] This includes any proposed regulation that is inconsistent with its enabling statute or with the Constitution, including the *Charter of Rights and Freedoms*.[26]

3. **Making.** This step is governed by the statute authorizing the regulation to be made, as well as the nature of the body making it. For example, Governor in Council regulations are made when the Governor General signs an order to that effect recommended by a Cabinet committee (the Treasury Board). The CRTC makes regulations through resolutions adopted at its meetings. Most provincial regulations are made by the lieutenant governor of the province on the recommendation of its Executive Council.[27] Similarly, in the territories, the commissioner makes regulations on the recommendation of the Executive Council or the relevant minister.[28]

4. **Registering or filing.** Most regulations are statutorily required to be registered or filed promptly in a registry system to keep track of them and facilitate access to them.[29] These requirements do not apply to some regulations, particularly those that are

made in large numbers and only apply to a narrow set of circumstances or entities, such as orders of the Canadian Wheat Board or Canadian Grain Commission, or certain types of permits.[30]

5. **Publishing.** Most regulations are statutorily required to be published in an official government publication called a *Gazette*.[31] They are also published online through government websites providing access to legislation such as the Justice Laws Website, as well as the website of the Canadian Legal Information Institute (CanLII).[32] Some exceptions apply, as they do for registration and filing.
6. **Parliamentary review.** In a few jurisdictions, regulations are subject to parliamentary review.[33] The most active review is conducted federally and in Ontario.

   The federal Standing Joint Committee for the Scrutiny of Regulations (SJCSR) is composed of senators and members of the House of Commons. Its mandate is to review all regulations after they are made on the basis of a set of criteria approved by both Houses.[34] These criteria include consistency with enabling legislation and infringement of rights. The SJCSR actively engages government ministers and departments, raising its concerns about the regulations they are responsible for.

   The SJCSR also has authority under section 19.1 of the *Statutory Instruments Act* to table a report containing a resolution that all or part of a regulation be revoked. This provision is rarely used but strengthens the influence of the SJCSR over entities to which Parliament has given regulation-making authority.

   The Legislative Assembly of Ontario is the only other legislative body in Canada with a committee for reviewing government regulations. The Standing Committee on Regulations and Private Bills is established by Standing Orders in accordance with section 33 of the *Legislation Act*.[35] Its role is to

   > examine the regulations with particular reference to the scope and method of the exercise of delegated legislative power but without reference to the merits of the policy or objectives to be effected by the regulations or enabling Acts.[36]

The committee reviews 500 to 600 regulations each year, raises its concerns with the ministries responsible for regulations, and occasionally reports regulations to the Legislative Assembly.[37] The Assembly has no authority to disallow regulations.

The Assemblies of Quebec, Manitoba, and Saskatchewan have disallowance authority, but they have no committees to systematically review executive legislation. Their disallowance authority has been rarely, if ever, exercised.[38]

Procedural Rules of Courts and Tribunals

Procedural rules govern how proceedings are initiated and conducted before courts and administrative tribunals. These rules serve many purposes, but they are basically intended to ensure legal proceedings are conducted in a just, fair, and efficient manner.[39]

Superior courts have inherent jurisdiction to regulate their proceedings, including by making general rules of procedure.[40] However, legislation dealing with courts also typically authorizes courts[41] or rules committees[42] to make rules of procedure. The committees are composed of judges, lawyers, and court officials. Rules for administrative tribunals are generally made by the tribunals.[43]

In many cases, procedural rules are also subject to approval by the government (Governor in Council or Lieutenant Governor in Council)[44] and are required to be registered and published in the same way as executive legislation (regulations).[45] They are included in online repositories of federal, provincial, and territorial laws.[46]

Municipal or Local Bylaws

Municipal or local bylaws are the most common form of delegated legislation. They are made under provincial legislation creating institutions to govern localities within a province or territory (regional districts, cities, towns, villages, and townships) and conferring powers on them to manage local matters. Most provinces have general legislation (usually known as municipal or local governance Acts) governing these institutions and authorizing them to make bylaws.[47] In addition, legislation may be enacted for particular localities providing additional powers, including power to make bylaws.[48]

Municipal or local bylaws are made by councils whose proceedings are open to the public and entail notice of meetings and debate, although the details of these processes are variable. For example, in Ontario, municipalities are required to pass procedure bylaws governing their meetings.[49] In contrast, the *Local Governance Act* of New Brunswick sets out bylaw-making procedures in some detail.[50]

There is also no uniform method of publishing municipal or local bylaws. They are not included in repositories of federal, provincial, or territorial laws. However, many municipalities make them available on their websites.[51]

PART TWO

Interpreting and Applying Legislation

CHAPTER FOUR

What Is Legislation Used For?

Legislation is used for many different purposes.

First of all, law-makers use it to govern the behaviour of people for social, economic, and environmental purposes, ideally for the public good. Legislation is the primary means by which elected bodies (Parliament and legislatures) do this. To be effective in this regard, legislation must express what law-makers want people to do and communicate this intention to them. This is why courts often refer to the "intention of Parliament." However, a parliamentary body consisting of many members cannot have an "intention" in the same way an individual can. Each member of the body can have their own intention about the legislation, but these intentions may vary substantially. The intention of Parliament is something analogous to individual intention; courts use the analogy to arrive at the meaning of a legislative text. It brings a legislator's perspective to understanding the meaning of the legislation. In *R v Secretary of State for the Environment, Transport and the Regions, Ex parte Spath Holme Ltd*, Lord Nicholls described legislation intention this way:

> The phrase is a shorthand reference to the intention which the court reasonably imputes to Parliament in respect of the language used. It is not the subjective intention of the minister or other

> persons who promoted the legislation. Nor is it the subjective intention of the draftsman, or of individual members or even of a majority of individual members of either House. These individuals will often have widely varying intentions. Their understanding of the legislation and the words used may be impressively complete or woefully inadequate.[1]

In turn, people use legislation to guide their behaviour. It applies to people generally according to its terms on an ongoing basis as long as it is in force.[2] It states rules of conduct they must follow. If they do not, they risk being subject to enforcement action government officials, courts, and administrative tribunals may take to require compliance.

Legislation also creates rights and powers, which entitle those who hold them to do things that affect other people. For example, if legislation entitles a person to be issued a licence, an official responsible for issuing licences must issue it and, once it is issued, the person is entitled to do what the licence authorizes and no one can legally stop them.

Legislation is also used to settle disputes between people who have different ideas about what they (or others) must (or must not) do, or about what they are entitled to do. These disputes often concern things that have already occurred, in which case legislation is used to determine what happens when things have not been done in accordance with the legislation (for example, imposing punishment or requiring the payment of damages).

How Is It Used? (Finding, Understanding, and Applying Legislation)

People use legislation by acquiring an understanding of what it means and then applying that understanding to their circumstances. Understanding legislation and applying it are distinct but closely related functions. Understanding is about learning what the legislation provides in general terms. Applying it involves drawing conclusions about how that general understanding affects (or not) particular circumstances.

The most basic way of acquiring an understanding of legislation is by reading it. More people than ever are doing this as legislation has become widely available online. However, there are still relatively few people who read it. Legislation guides people's conduct even when they have not read the legislation, but instead behave in accordance with their understanding of what the legislation requires. This is what happens most of the time. Most people acquire their understanding by learning about it through the media, government websites, or educational or licensing programs (for example, for driver's licences), or by obtaining advice from someone who understands it (for example, a legal practitioner or government official). These methods of acquiring an understanding of legislation all require someone to have located and read the legislation. Finding and reading it are at the core of how legislation functions and is used.

Finding relevant legislation can be challenging. Although access to legislation has improved remarkably with its online publication,[3] it is still not easy to find legislation relevant to particular circumstances. The titles of legislation provide some guidance to their subject matter, but there are often different ways of describing this subject matter. There is also a more recent trend toward titles that send political messages as opposed to informing people about the contents of the legislation.[4] And even when relevant legislation has been found, it is often difficult to locate the particular relevant provisions if the legislation is long and complex. Legal research skills are taught in law schools and are not easily acquired.[5]

This Part assumes the relevant legislative provisions have been located and focuses on reading and understanding them and applying that understanding to determine what should be done (or should have been done) in particular circumstances. There is often little difficulty in drawing conclusions about this. For example, if legislation requires the driver of an automobile to obey speed limits posted on highways, the driver can see both the signs and the speedometer and draw conclusions about how fast they should drive. However, there are many circumstances when it is more difficult to draw conclusions about what is required. In these circumstances, different people may draw different conclusions. But to guide people and settle disputes, legislation must convey a single meaning. It cannot mean whatever someone wants it to mean. The rule of law (which is a fundamental constitutional principle underlying Canada's legal system) requires the uniform application of the law to everyone. Legislation can, of course, contain different rules for different groups of people and situations. But the rules apply uniformly according to their terms.

Disputes about the meaning of legislation are prompted by disagreement about how it applies and the result of its application. People do not take disputes about meaning to court unless there is something else at stake. Resolving the meaning of the legislation is how the underlying disagreement is resolved.

Disputes about the meaning of legislation tend to focus on particular words in the legislation; there is no disagreement about what the other words of the legislation mean. For example, a dispute about whether employees were entitled to be paid benefits when their employer declared bankruptcy was resolved by focusing on the meaning of the word "termination" in employment standards legislation.[6] Everyone involved in the case agreed it depended on the meaning of this word. But it was the employees' claim to payment of the benefits that prompted the dispute, not their interest in the meaning of the word. The parties and the courts in this case spent little time discussing the meaning of the other words in the legislation, although as we will see below, they used some of these words to interpret "termination."

Why Is Legislation so Often Difficult to Understand?

There are many reasons to explain difficulties in understanding and applying legislation. These reasons do not necessarily justify this difficulty, but they explain why it persists.

Canadian legislative drafting practices are founded in the drafting traditions of England. A notable exception is the drafting of the *Civil Code* of Quebec, which is founded on somewhat different French traditions.

The style of legislative drafting when the English legal system implanted in Canada in the latter part of the eighteenth century was very detailed, using legalistic language, much of which was taken from Latin or French. This style originated with conveyancers who drafted documents dealing with property, such as deeds or leases. It made its way into legislation through constitutional developments in the institution of Parliament and the legislative process. Before the fifteenth century, Acts were drafted by judges on the instruction of the king in response to petitions from the Houses of Parliament. As these Houses acquired more control over the legislative process, they no longer presented petitions to the king, but rather bills setting out the details of the statute. Members of Parliament engaged conveyancers to draft the bills in a very detailed and legalistic fashion.[7]

A second reason has to do with the dominant interpretive approach taken by courts by the late eighteenth century and continuing into the twentieth.[8] They applied what was known as the literal rule of interpretation, focusing exclusively on the text and paying little attention to other features that have since come to be recognized as essential to interpreting legislation (as described below).[9] This approach seems to have been driven in large part by judicial resistance to legislation they viewed as an incursion on the common law or individual rights (particularly as the scope of legislation expanded beyond private matters to address broader social and economic concerns). This explains why penal and tax legislation are among the most difficult forms of legislation to understand. They are rooted in this older interpretive tradition and employ a very detailed style to overcome strict judicial interpretation that protects accused persons from imprisonment and taxpayers from paying taxes. Although the strictness of this interpretation has moderated since the latter part of the twentieth century, it continues to have some influence.[10]

A third reason is the increasing complexity of the matters legislation addresses, particularly as a result of technological development and the diversity of communities. We no longer live (if we ever did) in a world where social, economic, and environmental issues can be resolved by simple rules. The complexity of modern legislation reflects the complexity of life itself. This complexity poses challenges for anticipating how circumstances legislation addresses will unfold. Legislative drafting is about imagining the future, but this is a challenging task, especially in a complex and constantly changing world. This point has been most recently demonstrated by the flood of legislation made to deal with the COVID-19 pandemic. For example, the Ontario *Emergency Management and Civil Protection Act*[11] was initially used to address the pandemic, but within six months it was effectively replaced by another Act, the *Reopening Ontario (a Flexible Response to COVID-19) Act*.[12] In turn, these Acts were augmented by more than 100 regulations,[13] and many of them were themselves repeatedly amended to deal with the constantly changing nature of the pandemic.[14]

Courts have generally not been sympathetic to the difficulties people have in understanding and applying legislation. They continue to apply the maxim that ignorance of the law is no excuse and have largely rejected vagueness as a basis for invalidating or not applying legislation. In *Canadian Foundation for Children, Youth and the Law v Canada (Attorney General)*, the Supreme Court said:

> A law is unconstitutionally vague if it "does not provide an adequate basis for legal debate" and "analysis"; "does not sufficiently delineate any area of risk"; or "is not intelligible". The law must offer a "grasp to the judiciary" . . . Certainty is not required.[15]

This sets a high standard, met only when legislation is so unintelligible that lawyers and judges cannot develop legal arguments about its meaning. This threshold has been met only a handful of times in Canada.[16]

The difficulties described above persist in Canada, but the modern legislative drafting and interpretation practices described in this book have helped to alleviate them.

What Roles Do Legislators and Courts Have?

Legislators "make" legislation. Another word often used to describe this, particularly in relation to Acts, is "enact." But once legislation is made, legislators have no further role in its interpretation and application. This reflects another basic tenet of the rule of law: that legislation once made stands on its own as an expression of the law. Legislators cannot afterwards dictate what it means; their role is to approve its wording. Once approved, the words speak for themselves in accordance with the interpretive methodology described in the subsequent chapters.

Legislators can, however, make interpretive rules as part of the legislation they enact. For example, legislation frequently contains definitions of some of the terms it uses. Legislators have also made general legislation dealing with interpretation, most often called the Interpretation Act or the Legislation Act. These Acts contain definitions of terms that legislation frequently uses as well as rules for interpreting legislation. One of the most fundamental of these rules says legislation should be "given such fair, large and liberal construction and interpretation as best ensures the attainment of its objects."[17]

Although everyone who is subject to legislation is entitled to read and understand it, courts generally have the last word on what it means and how it applies in particular situations. This too reflects an important aspect of the rule of law: independent courts deciding matters impartially in accordance with the law. However, courts are also prepared to respect the views of administrative tribunals that interpret and apply legislation and will generally overturn their decisions only when they are unreasonable.[18]

Sometimes legislators are dissatisfied with how courts have interpreted their legislation. Although they cannot tell courts to change their decisions, they can change the legislation and express its intent more clearly. But after they have done so, it is again ultimately up to the courts to say what the changed legislation means and how it applies.

CHAPTER FIVE

How Is Legislation Understood and Applied?

Since courts resolve disputes about the meaning and application of legislation, the methodology they have developed for doing so should be applied by everyone. This methodology not only reflects the functions of legislation discussed above (particularly to achieve the policy goals of the bodies that make it and communicate its terms to those it affects), it is also connected to the role of language and the way legislation has been drafted.

Language

The functions of legislation are best advanced by enacting it in languages that are widely understood by both those who make the legislation and those who are subject to it. In Canada, these languages are English and French. In Nunavut, legislation is also enacted in the Inuit language. Indigenous languages are also used in the laws of self-governing Indigenous peoples.[1] These are known as natural languages and are recognized as fundamental for the social interaction that defines the linguistic communities that use them. In *Re Manitoba Language Rights*, the Supreme Court of Canada noted:

> [T]he essential role that language plays in human existence, development and dignity. It is through language that we are able to form concepts; to structure and order the world around us. Language bridges the gap between isolation and community, allowing humans to delineate the rights and duties they hold in respect of one another, and thus to live in society.[2]

Legislation is to be understood in the way it is understood by those who use it. This is often referred to as "ordinary meaning," which depends on the meaning attached to particular words by those who use the language, and the way words function together (grammar or syntax).

English and French have been widely understood in Canada since the country was formed under British rule. However, as natural languages, they evolve over time: many of today's words ("Wi-Fi") and usages ("text" as a verb meaning to send a text message) were unknown fifty years ago; and many words ("groovy") and usages ("far out," meaning "awesome") of fifty years ago are no longer current.

Natural languages are also prone to ambiguity (multiple different meanings) and vagueness (uncertainty about the scope of meaning). Ambiguity and vagueness are problems in the application of legislation. But legislation must apply uniformly according to its terms. If it is ambiguous, there must be a way to resolve it to a single meaning; if it is vague, there must be a way to establish the limits of its meaning. This is what interpretive methodology is about.

Drafting Practices

Legislation is not only written (drafted) in natural languages, it is also a unique form of writing. Like other forms, it has its own practices and conventions, which have developed over centuries. These practices and conventions are generally followed in the drafting of federal, provincial, and territorial legislation, but there are also variations. For example, in federal legislation, sections and subsections may be divided into "paragraphs," but in most provinces they are called "clauses."

There is a clear connection between legislative drafting and judicial interpretation. It emerges when one looks at their history. In England's earliest stages as a country after the Norman Conquest, it was difficult to say what legislation was. Parliament as we know it today did not exist. The king issued a variety of legal instruments, that might or might not have had legislative effect.[3] Some of them resulted from petitions presented to the king by his councils (which eventually developed into the Houses of Parliament). If the king accepted a petition, it would be drafted into an Act by judges of the king's court. Because the judges had drafted them and considered they knew what they were supposed to say, they adopted a purposive approach, paying less attention to the words and instead focusing on the "mischief" the legislation was supposed to address.[4] A judge during this period is reported to have said, "Do not gloss [interpret] the statute. We know better than you for we made it."[5]

Drafting by the king's judges lasted until the fifteenth century. At this point, the Houses of Parliament had been established and began to assert greater control over the law-making process by presenting draft Acts (bills) to the king rather than petitions.[6] They employed land lawyers (conveyancers) to draft the bills, whose drafting style was very detailed and verbose. The purposive interpretive approach gave way to what is known as strict or literal interpretation. It put more emphasis on the wording of the legislation, even when it seemed inconsistent with the purposes.[7] By the beginning of the nineteenth century, literal interpretation was prevalent, but it was later moderated by what became known as the "Golden Rule" of interpretation.[8] It involved applying the "ordinary" or "plain" meaning of legislation unless it resulted in an "absurdity."[9]

Around the middle of the nineteenth century, the drafting of Acts of the British Parliament was entrusted to specialist drafters called parliamentary counsel. The Office of Parliamentary Counsel was established in 1869 under Lord Thring, who in 1887 published a treatise on legislative drafting entitled *Practical Legislation*.[10] It set out rules for arranging the contents of legislation and for drafting sentences and particular types of provisions. Although it was not the first work on drafting legislation, it had considerable influence in England and beyond.

In Canada, the Uniform Law Conference recognized the importance of legislative drafting and the need to improve it at the first meeting of the Conference in 1918.[11] The Report of the Committee on Legislative Drafting pieced together extracts from seven British and American texts on legislative drafting (including Lord Thring's), highlighting practices in stark contrast to the prevailing style of the nineteenth century. They advocated consistent word use, brevity, and short sentences in the active voice and present tense; they admonished the use of legalistic words and provisos. After the Second World War, EA Driedger brought greater attention to this approach with law journal articles,[12] the publication of *The Composition of Legislation* in 1957,[13] and his influence as a legislative counsel and deputy minister in the federal Department of Justice, and later as a professor at the University of Ottawa.

Today, the publication of texts on legislative drafting continues[14] and the Drafting Conventions of the Uniform Law Conference of Canada encapsulate a plainer, simpler approach that aligns with the Plain Language Movement[15] of the late twentieth century:

> **Style**
>
> 2. An Act should be written simply, clearly and concisely, with the required degree of precision, and as much as possible in ordinary language. Simplicity and conciseness of language can be made to exist with precision in a well organized text. It is important not to exaggerate the degree of precision that is required.[16]

These texts and conventions have largely been followed in drafting federal, provincial, and territorial legislation in Canada. The exceptions consist mainly of penal and tax legislation where older drafting practices persist.

Driedger's Modern Principle of Interpretation: Text, Context, and Purposes

Driedger not only drafted and wrote about drafting, he also studied the interpretive methodology of the courts in Canada and the United Kingdom. His work on interpretation has had an enormous influence in Canada. In 1976, he published *The Construction of Statutes*, which synthesized the various judicial approaches into his Modern Principle:

> [T]he words of an Act are to be read in their entire context and in their grammatical and ordinary sense harmoniously with the scheme of the Act, the object of the Act, and the intention of Parliament.[17]

This principle resonates with modern legislative drafting practices and has been overwhelmingly adopted by Canadian courts, particularly since the decision of the Supreme Court of Canada in *Re Rizzo & Rizzo Shoes Ltd.*[18] It is also incorporated into the Model Interpretation Act of the Uniform Law Conference of Canada:

> **Enactment remedial**
>
> 10 (1) The words of an Act and regulations authorized under an Act are to be read in their entire context, and in their grammatical and ordinary sense, harmoniously with the scheme of the Act, the object of the Act and the intention of Parliament.
>
> (2) Acts and regulations are to be construed as being remedial and are to be given the fair, large and liberal interpretation that best ensures the attainment of their objects.[19]

This rule has now been enacted in section 2-10 of the Saskatchewan *Legislation Act*.[20]

The modern principle emphasizes three aspects of interpretation:

1. *the words*, which are to be read *in their grammatical and ordinary sense*;
2. *their entire context*; and
3. *the scheme . . . the object*, and *the intention of Parliament*.[21]

Canadian courts frequently discuss these aspects under the headings of *text*, *context*, and *purpose*. The Supreme Court has most recently affirmed this approach in *Canada v Vavilov*:

> [118] This Court has adopted the "modern principle" as the proper approach to statutory interpretation, because legislative intent can be understood only by reading the language chosen by the legislature in light of the purpose of the provision and the entire relevant context. . . . Those who draft and enact statutes expect that questions about their meaning will be resolved by an analysis that has regard to the text, context and purpose.[22]

The three aspects of text, context, and purpose are interconnected.

The "text" is composed of the words being interpreted (words whose meaning will determine the issues to be resolved by applying legislation). The text cannot be understood without understanding the linguistic context of the language in which it is drafted. Languages associate meanings with words (lexical) and determine how the words work together (grammar or syntax). But language is so intimately connected with the text that its role is treated as part of textual analysis.

Other contextual features also contribute to understanding the text. For example, words surrounding the text affect their meaning, as indeed do other provisions of the legislation containing the text, and other legislation as well. These and other contextual features affect the meaning of the text.[23]

Purposes also affect the meaning of the text, much as the contextual features do. But textual and contextual features also have a bearing on what the purposes are. Purposes are often determined by reading the text and its contextual provisions, or by considering the events surrounding its enactment.[24]

The interconnection of text, context, and purpose is also signalled in the Driedger principle's reference to "harmoniously." Courts have assumed legislators intend their laws to be coherent and consistent, not only internally, but also with each other, with the Constitution, and with generally accepted legal principles, such as natural justice in government decision-making. Coherence and consistency are determined using rules of logic as well as the legislative purposes, which are in turn determined by looking at contextual features.[25]

An important feature about this interpretive methodology is that it does not depend on a single interpretive rule or consideration. It underscores the fact that the so-called rules of interpretation are seldom hard and fast rules (if indeed they are rules at all) and that interpretation is not a matter of applying rules with mathematical precision. Rather, it results from looking at a range of interpretive features and considering them together. It is a way of reasoning, not a calculation.

The discussion that follows adopts the tri-partite structure described above. Text is discussed first since words are the starting point for understanding meaning. Purpose is discussed next because it fundamentally orients that meaning — meaning must be consistent with purposes. Finally, context is discussed because it informs the meaning of the text and is used to determine purposes.

CHAPTER SIX

Legislative Text

Canadian courts have accepted that (as stated in EA Driedger's Modern Principle of Interpretation) words in legislation are to be read in their ordinary and grammatical sense. This refers to the meaning they have both as individual words (lexical) as well as in relationship to each other in groups (sentences, clauses, and phrases) as a matter of grammar or syntax. The sentence, "The hunter eats shoots and leaves" illustrates lexical ambiguity in that *shoots* and *leaves* can be verbs or nouns. Syntactic ambiguity is illustrated by the Groucho Marx quip: "This morning I shot an elephant in my pyjamas. How he got into my pyjamas, I dunno."

Lexical Analysis

The courts presume law-makers intend their words to be understood in their ordinary sense. This has both a practical and a legal basis. Practically speaking, using words in their ordinary sense is an effective means of communicating to a wide audience. Legally speaking, the maxim "ignorance of the law is no excuse" assumes people are capable of understanding the law and must do so. Legislation written in language to be understood in its ordinary sense supports this assumption.

However, there is an exception to the ordinary meaning approach: words with a technical meaning (including legal meaning) will be given that meaning instead. It too responds to the need to communicate effectively with those whom the legislation affects; it applies when legislation deals with technical matters likely to concern only a small portion of the general public. This section considers each of these types of meaning and then looks at how groups of words are interpreted.

Ordinary Meaning

Ruth Sullivan has characterized ordinary meaning in legislation as:

> [T]he reader's first impression meaning, the understanding that spontaneously comes to mind when words are read in their immediate context — in the words of Gonthier, J, "the natural meaning which appears when the provision is simply read through."[1]

The reader referred to here is an "ordinary reader" or, as Sullivan elsewhere describes this person, a "competent language user."[2] However, this notion of ordinary meaning is as complex as language itself and entails many variabilities. When interpreting and applying legislation, it cannot be determined simply by asking yourself what words mean to you.

The meaning and usage of words in a particular language often vary from one place to another. English in Canada is not exactly the same as in the United Kingdom or the United States. For example, different words are used for many parts of an automobile (a "trunk" in Canada is a "boot" in the United Kingdom; "pop" in Canada is "soda" in the United States). Variations also exist within Canada (a "cottage" in southern Ontario is a "camp" in Quebec and northern Ontario).

Words most often have more than one possible meaning, as a glance through any dictionary demonstrates. Although their possible meanings are often related, they sometimes have quite different meanings (for example, a "file" can be either a tool for reducing the size of something or a place for putting documents).

Words can also have different grammatical functions (as noted above in the example of "eats shoots and leaves"). Many of them can be nouns, verbs, and adjectives (for example, a "file" is a place for documents, "file" is the action of putting a document there, and "*file* manager" is someone who keeps track of files).

All these variabilities present challenges to understanding words in legislation. Dictionaries can help sort out these challenges by offering authoritative examples of how words are or have been used in particular contexts. But care must be taken because dictionaries are geographically focused. A definition of a word in a dictionary of English in the United States or the United Kingdom will not necessarily apply in Canada. A Canadian dictionary should be used when reading Canadian legislation.[3]

Courts have generally resisted attempts to introduce evidence of ordinary meaning.[4] Judges rely on their own understanding of language and may also take judicial notice of ordinary meaning as a factual matter that is "so notorious or accepted as not to be the subject of debate" or is "capable of immediate and accurate demonstration by resort to accessible sources of indisputable accuracy."[5] Courts also consider dictionaries, which provide possible meanings, but do not resolve what a word means in a particular piece of legislation. This is why it is essential to consider the context in which a word is used. Context is what most often resolves questions about which meaning a word is intended to have. It may also open the door to evidence related to the meaning of words.[6]

Technical Meaning

Although courts presume words in legislation are intended to have ordinary meaning, they have created an exception for legislation that deals with technical matters.[7] This exception recognizes that not all legislation is widely applicable. Some of it deals with matters involving people who have developed specialized language to communicate among themselves about these matters. It assumes they are the principal audience for the legislation. Medical matters are a good example. Medical practitioners have developed an extensive vocabulary unique to their practices. It allows them to communicate more precisely and efficiently than if they had to use ordinary language.

Some words have only a technical meaning: there is no ordinary (generally understood) meaning to apply. These words are interpreted in the sense they have within that community. For example, a medical term such as *cardioversion* will be given the meaning a cardiologist would give it (a procedure for restoring the normal rhythm of the heart by applying mild electric shocks). Courts determine the meaning of these terms on the basis of expert evidence from members of the technical community.[8]

Some words have both ordinary and technical meanings. Courts assume the ordinary meaning was intended and require convincing counter-arguments before they will apply a technical meaning,[9] even when legislation deals with technical or scientific matters.[10] For example, the word "derivative" in relation to a substance has an ordinary meaning of a substance physically derived from another. In the pharmaceutical industry, "derivative" has been understood as extending to substances "of a similar group" or that have "similar characteristics."[11] However, in *Pfizer Co Ltd v Deputy Minister of National Revenue*, the Supreme Court applied the ordinary meaning of this word when used in legislation imposing duties on imported pharmaceutical products.[12] The decision is puzzling because the legislation dealt with a technical matter (manufacturing pharmaceutical products), but it was a taxation statute applying to importation (an activity not requiring any special expertise). Other courts have reached similar conclusions.[13]

Although the *Pfizer* decision suggests a strong presumption in favour of ordinary meaning, this concept has been nuanced when legislation, or specific provisions, apply to a particular group of people or subject matter.[14] In these cases, courts have concluded the meaning to be applied is "that sense which people conversant with the subject matter ... would attribute to it."[15] This approach has been applied in some Canadian cases,[16] but it has also been recently rejected by the Federal Court of Appeal in a case, like *Pfizer*, involving import duties.[17]

Legal Meaning

Legal meaning arises either from legislative provisions that stipulate meaning (interpretation provisions) or from the practice of judges and lawyers, particularly as recognized in the common law. It is different from other technical meaning in that it has been developed by the very people who are concerned with its interpretation in legislation (law-makers and legal practitioners). No outside expert evidence is needed to prove its meaning in court. Judges and lawyers are the experts.

This might also explain why courts have not applied the presumption of ordinary meaning to legal meaning in the same way they have for other technical meaning. In fact, the Supreme Court in *R v DLW* has suggested there is a presumption in favour of legal meaning:

> [W]hen Parliament uses a legal term with a well-understood legal meaning, it is presumed that Parliament intended to incorporate that legal meaning into the statute. . . . [A]ny departure from that legal meaning must be clear, either by express language or necessary implication from the statute.[18]

This reflects the fact that the practice of law is a specialized matter, like the practice of other professions or disciplines. And it has been largely assumed to require specialized language to operate. However, law is different from other technical subjects and disciplines insofar as people generally are supposed to understand it and conduct themselves accordingly. In addition, access to courts and tribunals to advance views about the meaning and application of law is recognized as a constitutional right.[19] But access to legal services is limited by costs: many people are unable to afford legal representation and unrepresented litigants are now common in many courts, particularly those dealing with family or criminal law. This calls into question the degree to which legislation dealing with legal matters should use legal language that most of the public does not understand, and why words having both ordinary and legal meaning must be given their legal meaning.

Some courts have responded to this concern by revising their rules of practice to reduce the use of legal language, particularly Latin expressions. For example, the Ontario *Rules of Civil Procedure* now use "without notice" instead of "*ex parte.*"[20] However, revision of this sort can be difficult. If a term is used in many pieces of legislation, its replacement in some places but not others may raise questions about consistency of meaning. This difficulty becomes even greater when terminology is also used in private law documents such as contracts and deeds. In these cases, fairly extensive legislative measures are required to make language more accessible. Notable examples are the *Short Form of Leases Act* and the *Land Registration Reform Act*, which simplified legal language used in documents for leasing or transferring real property.[21] More modest, but far more generally applicable, reforms have also been made in the revision of statutes, notably in British Columbia in 1996 as a result of calls for more accessible legislation and plainer language.[22]

When access to justice and more recent drafting and legislative changes to widen the understandability legislation are taken into account, it should be more (not less) difficult to displace the presumption of ordinary meaning.

Meaning Developed by Courts and Legal Practitioners

As with other technical meaning, legal meaning has been developed by the professionals who use it (courts and legal practitioners) as part of the common law and court procedure. The common law is a legal system originating with the courts established by Henry II in the twelfth century. One of the functions of these courts was to harmonize the disparate legal systems that had previously existed in England and produce a "common" law.[23] Practitioners who engaged in non-litigious aspects of legal practice, such as drafting wills or deeds of property, also developed terminology, often based on earlier legal systems such as Roman law.

As with other technical language, some terms have only a legal meaning (for example, "tort" or "mortgage") while others also have ordinary meaning (for example, "right," "costs," or "discovery"). The passage quoted above from *R v DLW* suggests courts assume legislators intend the legal meaning,[24] including for words with dual meaning. However, this is not an ironclad assumption. In *Will-Kare Paving & Contracting Ltd v Canada*,[25] the Supreme Court held that "sale" had a legal meaning, while in *Celgene Corp v Canada* it applied the ordinary meaning of "sold."[26] In *Celgene*, the Court concluded the purposes of the legislation favoured the ordinary meaning, whereas in *Will-Kare*, the majority was not persuaded there was any reason to depart from the legal meaning. This is one of the many examples of how the interpretation of legislation seldom if ever depends on applying a single interpretive factor. It always results from a combination of interpretive considerations.

Legislated Meaning

The potential for legal meaning to hamper the accessibility of legislation diminishes when that meaning is legislated. The legal meaning can be explained in the legislation itself, for example, through definitions.

In Canada, definitions are usually near the beginning of a legislative text, although they may also be elsewhere when the defined words are used only in a few provisions. They are also included in general interpretation legislation (an Interpretation Act or Legislation Act). These definitions apply to the meaning of words in all legislation "unless a contrary intention appears" or their application "would give to a term or provision a meaning that is inconsistent with the context."[27]

Interpretation or Legislation Acts define words and phrases that occur frequently in legislation, such as "Governor in Council," "person," or "holiday." For example, subsection 35(1) of the Canada

Interpretation Act contains over fifty generally applicable definitions, and section 87 of the Ontario *Legislation Act, 2006* contains nineteen.

There are two types of definitions differentiated by the verbs they use.

Definitions that say terms "mean" something are exhaustive. They apply only to the extent of the meaning they describe and exclude any other meaning.[28]

Definitions saying terms "include" something are non-exhaustive. They do not exclude other, ordinary meanings associated with the terms. Sometimes definitions combine these formulations, defining terms exhaustively but also including particular things, usually to avoid doubts about whether the exhaustive part of the definition includes them.

Definitions are not the only way legislatures can determine the meaning of the words they use in legislation. Provisions can also be enacted to deal with the way words are to be interpreted. For example, most Interpretation Acts in Canada contain provisions similar to section 33 of the federal *Interpretation Act*:

> **Gender**
>
> 33 (1) Words importing female persons include male persons and corporations and words importing male persons include female persons and corporations.[29]
>
> **Number**
>
> (2) Words in the singular include the plural, and words in the plural include the singular.
>
> **Parts of speech and grammatical forms**
>
> (3) Where a word is defined, other parts of speech and grammatical forms of the same word have corresponding meanings.

Other interpretive rules extend the application of definitions in one piece of legislation to other legislation "relating to the same subject."[30]

Another way meaning can be legislated is through declaratory legislation. As the name suggests, it is legislation that "declares" that a particular provision has a particular meaning. It can also apply more generally to the interpretation of a particular enactment. Legislatures use these provisions in two circumstances.

The first is to avoid doubts about the meaning of a provision when it is being enacted. These declaratory provisions usually begin with the phrase "for greater certainty" and add precision, often either including or excluding particular meanings. For example, the *Canadian Energy Regulator Act* contains the following declaratory provisions:

> **Rights of Indigenous peoples of Canada**
>
> 3 For greater certainty, nothing in this Act is to be construed as abrogating or derogating from the protection provided for the rights of the Indigenous peoples of Canada by the recognition and affirmation of those rights in section 35 of the *Constitution Act, 1982*.
>
> . . .
>
> **Clarification**
>
> 42 (2) For greater certainty, the power referred to in subsection (1) includes the power to designate a single member, including the Lead Commissioner, as the sole commissioner who is authorized to deal with the application.[31]

The second circumstance is when the courts have arrived at an interpretation of a provision that the legislature considers it did not intend. In these cases, the provision usually uses the word "declare" to stipulate the meaning. For example, in 2008 the National Assembly of Quebec enacted two new provisions (sections 14.1 and 228.1 of the *Supplemental Pensions Plan Act*) to clearly authorize the *Régie des rentes* to do something the Court of Appeal had said was not authorized by the legislation.[32] The amending Act included the following provision referring to the new provisions:

> 319.1 Sections 14.1 and 228.1 are declaratory.[33]

The Supreme Court of Canada held this created a "declaratory" provision and said:

> The interpretation imposed by a declaratory provision stretches back in time to the date when the legislation it purports to interpret

first came into force, with the effect that the legislation in question is deemed to have always included this provision.[34]

Syntactic Analysis

Legislative sentences have historically been very long and convoluted. This is the product of thinking that putting a series of ideas together in a single sentence will make clear their relationships to each other. Dividing them into separate sentences was thought to disrupt these connections and create ambiguity.

Today, the opposite is recognized to be true. Jumbling ideas together in one sentence is far more apt to result in ambiguity than dividing them into separate sentences. This is because of the flexibility of English in terms of word order and the grammatical character of words. A single word can be two or more parts of speech. For example, "file" can be a noun (a place to put documents), an adjective (a modifier of a noun related to files such as a "file folder"), or a verb (the action of putting something in a file). Also, related words and phrases can be strung together with a conjunction ("and" or "or") before the last one, but it may not be clear which words and phrases are conjoined and the nature of the relationship (conjunctive, disjunctive, or both) may not be clear. Ambiguity can be exposed by considering the grammatical character of each word and its possible relationship(s) to other words.

The following example from a case dealing with subsection 202(1) of the *Criminal Code* illustrates the potential for syntactic ambiguity and how the ambiguity can be explained. This subsection says:

> 202 (1) Every one commits an offence who
>
> . . .
>
> (b) imports, makes, buys, sells, rents, leases, hires or keeps, exhibits, employs or knowingly allows to be kept, exhibited or employed in any place under his control any device or apparatus for the purpose of recording or registering bets or selling a pool, or any machine or device for gambling or betting.[35]

The interpretive question this raised in *R v Volante* was whether it was an offence for someone who owned a gambling machine to keep it for public use in a café owned by someone else.[36] It is not easy to answer this question with a simple reading of the provision, which was drafted in the detailed style of drafting that prevailed in the nineteenth century. The ambiguities lurking here can be identified (as set out in the parentheses) as follows:

- *every one* (principal subject)
  - » *commits* (principal verb)
  - » *an offence* (object of the principal clause)
- *who* (subject of subordinate clause modifying the principal subject)
  - » imports, makes, buys, sells, rents, leases, hires (verbs in the subordinate clause)
  - » ***or*** (conjunction — **but what does it join?**)
  - » *keeps, exhibits, employs* (more verbs in the subordinate clause)
  - » ***or*** (another conjunction — **but what does it join?**)
  - » *knowingly* (adverb) *allows to be kept, exhibited or employed* (more verbs in the subordinate clause)
- ***in any place under his control*** (adverbial phrase modifying verbs in the subordinate clause — **but which ones?**)
- *any device or apparatus* (objects of the subordinate clause)
- ***for the purpose of recording or registering bets or selling a pool*** (prepositional phrase modifying something — **but what?**)
- *or* (conjunction joining *any device or apparatus*)
- *any machine or device for gambling or betting* (more objects of the subordinate clause).

Two ambiguities arise here. The first concerns what the phrase ***in any place under his control*** modifies. Does it modify:

- only the third group of verbs (allows to be kept, exhibited, or employed)?
- the second and third groups of verbs?
- all three groups of verbs?

The second ambiguity concerns what the phrase ***for the purpose of recording or registering bets or selling a pool*** modifies. Does it modify:

- the noun phrase "any device or apparatus"?
- the verbs in the subordinate clause?

This syntactical analysis frames these questions, but it does not answer them. To answer them, further interpretive factors, notably those relating to purpose and context, must be considered.

Textual Inferences

Many types of logical inferences are recognized in reading documents generally, and legislation in particular. In legislative interpretation, many of them have been labelled "maxims," "canons," or "rules" with Latin names reflecting their origins in Roman law. But their influence on interpretation is far from absolute. Although they can have a significant effect on the interpretation, they are not hard and fast rules. They often give way to other interpretive considerations, which is why it is apt to call them "inferences." The principal ones are discussed below under the following headings:

- Tautology
- Groups of Words or Phrases
- Consistent Meaning
- Implied Exclusion

Tautology

Both drafting and interpretive practices recognize that legislation should not repeat itself. It is not rhetorical speech, attempting to persuade. It states provisions having the force of law. It need say something only once to have legal effect; if it states something else, it must mean something else.

The Supreme Court of Canada has recognized an interpretive presumption against tautology countless times. Most recently, in

Canada v Canada North Group Inc,[37] it held that the list of examples in a definition of "security interest" in subsection 224(1.3) of the *Income Tax Act*[38] limited its scope so as to exclude super-priority charges under the *Companies' Creditors Arrangement Act*.[39]

Courts will not ignore words in legislation simply because they make it harder to administer legislation or apply its other provisions. In *Woods (Re)*, the court concluded that words giving a person the right to consent to a videoconference hearing (as opposed to a hearing in person) had to be adhered to, even during a health emergency when in-person hearings were prohibited.[40]

This inference of textual logic does not always prevail. Legislative provisions are sometimes added to clarify others (often including the words "for greater certainty") or to declare a particular meaning.[41] And, on rare occasions, other interpretive factors convince a court that provisions have no meaningful function. For example, in *Abakhan & Associates Inc v Braydon Investments Ltd*, the British Columbia Court of Appeal held that the words "by collusion, guile, malice or fraud" in section 1 of the *Fraudulent Conveyances Act*[42] added nothing to this section, which already spoke of "delay, hinder or defraud creditors and others of their just and lawful remedies."[43]

Groups of Words or Phrases

Groups of words or phrases that perform the same grammatical function are assumed to have something in common. This is exemplified in the *Canada North Group* case mentioned above. The definition of "security interest" in subsection 224(1.3) of the *Income Tax Act*[44] was framed in terms of a list of legal instruments made for the benefit of those who held them.[45] The Court concluded that "super-priority charges" under the *Companies' Creditors Arrangement Act*[46] did not fall within this definition since they were intended to benefit creditors as a group, and not particular persons.[47]

Another example is a case dealing with a provision creating an offence based on actions described in a series of verbs: "removes, conceals or disposes of ... property." In *R v Goulis*, the accused was charged with an offence based on this provision after having failed to disclose property as required in bankruptcy proceedings.[48] The main issue was whether this amounted to "conceals" property. The court decided it did not because the associated words ("removes" and "disposes") both required some positive action rather than simply a failure to do something.

The influence of groups of words or phrases on each other should not be overstated. Each of them must have some distinct significance (as just noted in the discussion of tautology). And if they are conjoined by the disjunctive "or," they cannot be fused into a single idea.[49]

Groups of words or phrases are frequently followed by a generic reference to "other" things. The generic reference takes its content from the preceding words and phrases. It includes things belonging to the class of things they describe. This class is determined by what these things have in common. For example, *Walker v Ritchie* concerned a court rule about awarding court costs.[50] The rule set out a series of matters for a court to consider. The last one was "(i) any *other* matter relevant to the question of costs." In *Walker v Ritchie*, the court considered whether the risk of non-payment of plaintiff's fees fell into the generic category. It began by identifying two elements the other matters had in common:

1) They could apply either to plaintiffs or defendants
2) They addressed either the nature of the case or the conduct of the parties, both of which could be assessed by either party

The court concluded the risk of non-payment of plaintiff's fees did not have these elements since it involved only the plaintiff (and not the defendant) and it could not be assessed by the defendant since it depended on a confidential relationship between the plaintiff and their lawyer.[51]

Consistent Meaning

Most words have a range of possible meanings, many of which may be quite different. If a word is used in a variety of different senses in a piece of legislation, it raises questions about which sense is intended each time it is used. Using words or expressions in the same sense throughout simplifies the task of interpretation and reduces disputes about meaning.

The interpretive presumption of consistent meaning reflects this: words or expressions are assumed to have the same meaning throughout a piece of legislation. And, correspondingly, different words or expressions are assumed to have different meanings. For example, the authority to "permit" someone to be physically absent from a hearing is different from authority to "order" attendance by videoconference. The one implies a right to attend in person (which can be waived), while the other does not imply that right.[52]

Although the inference of consistent meaning is most often applied, it does not apply when "a contrary intention appears."[53] This might occur when a word is defined in one way for the purposes of one part of the legislation, and differently for another part.[54]

Implied Exclusion

Implied exclusion (*expressio unius est exclusio alterius*) is one of the most frequently invoked textual inferences. Its application is also often rejected (particularly when there are doubts about the drafting quality of the legislation), suggesting it is a somewhat uncertain guide to meaning.[55] Much depends on the circumstances in which it is considered.

Implied exclusion is rooted in the assumption of precise expression with no tautology. Words denote the ideas they express, but that denotation is limited to things associated with the words. If something more had been intended, something more would have been said. The use of particular words impliedly excludes meaning that is not associated with them. For example, a reference to adverse possession "by abutting landowners" excluded adverse possession by anyone else.[56]

A second circumstance in which implied exclusion is applied is when legislation contains similar provisions, but some include additional wording not found in the others. For example, when an Act confers rule-making powers on two different bodies but requires the rules of only one of them to be approved by someone else, the other body is not subject to the approval requirement.[57] This aspect of implied exclusion can also apply across the statute book when similar provisions are in different statutes.[58]

Ruth Sullivan has suggested implied exclusion will apply whenever readers would expect to see something mentioned if it were intended.[59] These expectations can be discerned in patterns or practices of express reference. The circumstance just described of references in some comparable provisions, but not others, exemplifies this. For example, in *R v BG*, the court considered provisions of the *Criminal Code* allowing victims of crime to "appear and make submissions."[60] The court concluded this did not extend to the cross-examination of witnesses since this right is expressly conferred in other provisions of the *Code*.[61]

The application of implied exclusion depends on the legislative text having been drafted concisely in accordance with the no tautology principle. It may also give way in the face of difficulties in expressing legislative intent clearly. Thus, courts have discounted its value in the face of doubts about the drafting of the legislative text and the need to express details to set aside doubts about its meaning.[62]

Multilingual Legislation

When more than one language is spoken by a significant portion of the population, legislation is often required to be enacted in more than one language. In Canada, this is the case with federal legislation as well as the legislation of six provinces and territories, which are required to be enacted in both English and French. Not only must the enacted version be in both languages, but both languages must also be used in the enactment process such that proposed legislation is in both languages. In addition, both versions of the legislation have the same legal force: they are "equally authentic" and entitled to equal consideration when they are being applied.[63] Many of these requirements are constitutional,[64] while others are based on non-constitutional legislation.[65]

Legislation in Nunavut may also be enacted in the Inuit language[66] and legislation enacted under some Aboriginal self-government agreements may be in Indigenous languages.[67]

Multilingual legislation is more accessible to the linguistic communities it speaks to, but it also poses an additional interpretive challenge in terms of uniform expression of law. All language versions must say the same thing. This can be challenging since different languages operate differently and words in one language do not often have exact equivalents in other languages. In addition, the ambiguities to which one language is prone are multiplied when legislation is enacted in two or more languages having their own potential ambiguities.

Canadian courts have developed a methodology for interpreting bilingual (English-French) legislation to mean the same thing in both languages. It is founded on a presumption that when different interpretations are possible in the two languages, the meaning shared between them is the one intended.[68] The differences must be substantive; different ways of saying the same thing do not amount to different meaning.[69]

If one version is capable of two different meanings, but the other is capable of only one of them, the meaning they have in common is presumed to be intended. For example, in *R v Daoust*, the Supreme Court considered a list of prohibited actions relating to property. The English version included an action ("or otherwise deals with" property) that was not included in the French version. The French version expressed the narrower, shared meaning, which the Court then applied.[70]

The presumption of shared meaning is not conclusive and cannot in any case apply when there is no shared meaning (each version says something different from the other). Interpretation must go on to consider what meaning is supported by the purposes and context of the legislation.[71] For example, in *Canada (Citizenship and Immigration) v Khosa*, the English version of the *Federal Courts Act*[72] granted the Federal Court discretion to grant relief when certain grounds existed on judicial review, while the French version required the relief to be granted.[73] The Supreme Court found the English version more consistent with the discretionary nature of judicial review and applied that version as being consistent with this context and the purposes it inferred.

CHAPTER SEVEN

Purposes

Purposes are important elements of all communication. It is often difficult to answer a question without knowing why it is being asked. A simple question such as "Do you have a driver's licence?" might be asked to verify any number of things ranging from identity or age to the capacity to operate a motor vehicle. And when words have different possible meanings, the purposes underlying their use can help determine which meaning is intended.[1] It is not surprising that the purposes of legislation have a long history of guiding its interpretation. Their use has also been reinforced by provisions in Interpretation or Legislation Acts, such as section 12 of the federal *Interpretation Act*:

> **Enactments deemed remedial**
> **12** Every enactment is deemed remedial, and shall be given such fair, large and liberal construction and interpretation as best ensures the attainment of its objects.[2]

The use of purposes to interpret legislation is rooted in the primary role of legislators who make legislation to achieve purposes they consider to be in the public interest. Legislative interpretation must take these purposes into account. However, as Driedger's Modern Principle on Interpretation suggests, purposes are not the only interpretive consideration.[3] They must work "harmoniously" with the textual and contextual features of the legislation.[4] The concept of plausibility limits meaning to what "the words of the text can reasonably bear."[5] And contextual elements often bear on determining what the purposes are.

As a general matter, the broader the wording used in a legislative text, the more scope there is for purposes to affect its meaning. This is particularly true of constitutional legislation. Cases interpreting the division of legislative powers in sections 91 and 92 of the *Constitution Act, 1867*[6] and the *Canadian Charter of Rights and Freedoms*[7] give great consideration to their purposes and to the purposes of the legislative provisions being examined for conformity with these constitutional provisions.[8]

There are two aspects to considering purposes. The first is determining what the purposes are, or more precisely, what purposes have a bearing on the words being interpreted. The second is considering how those purposes affect the meaning of the words: do they tend toward an expansive or restrictive interpretation?

Purposes are used to choose among competing possible meanings a legislative text may have. This can entail, for example, deciding whether words should be given their ordinary meaning or a legal meaning[9] or how broadly or narrowly they should be interpreted.[10] Purposes, including those drawn from contextual elements, can also reveal ambiguities in a text that, when read in isolation, appears to be clear.[11]

Multiplicity of Purposes

Most legislation has multiple purposes operating at different levels of generality and focusing on different aspects of the legislation. Some purposes focus on what the legislation is trying to achieve in terms of public policy goals. They may relate to the entire legislative text, or they may be focused on particular provisions.

For example, the general purposes of the Ontario *Highway Traffic Act* are to promote road safety (prevent accidents) and the efficient use of roadways (avoid traffic jams and obstructions).[12] But the purpose of Part III.1 of the Act dealing with electric vehicle charging stations is to promote the use of electric vehicles for environmental purposes by prohibiting non-electric vehicles from being parked at these stations.

Other purposes relate to the functioning of the legislation itself. For example, the purpose of enforcement provisions creating offences or authorizing search and seizure is to ensure the effectiveness of the legislation in achieving its broader purposes.

Purposes can also be framed as principles or policies, providing general guidance on the administration of legislation.[13]

Purposes are not always consistent with each other and tensions may result between them. For example, one purpose of freedom of information legislation is to promote transparency of government operations, but another is to facilitate the role of public servants to provide advice to government ministers. The interpretive challenge is to find a balance between the competing purposes.[14]

Determining Purposes

Determining the purposes of legislation is a potentially complex task given the range of matters bearing on what they are. Courts rely on a variety of sources to determine these purposes.[15]

The most basic way to determine purposes is simply to consider what the text is dealing with and what it says about it, and infer why it was enacted. For example, it can be inferred that the purpose of legislation limiting the speed of motor vehicles is to prevent traffic accidents that become more likely and more dangerous as speed increases. This conclusion flows from an understanding of motor vehicle traffic and the risks it entails. This might be described as a matter of common sense, although care must be taken when invoking this concept that the sense really is "common."

Purposes may also be inferred from the legislation as a "whole" or the "scheme of the legislation," which is composed of the various provisions of the legislation and how they are organized and relate to one another. For example, in *Cuthbertson v Rasouli*, the Supreme Court considered the scheme of the Ontario *Health Care Consent Act, 1996*[16] to determine whether the Act applied to the withdrawal of medical treatment.[17] Both the majority and dissenting judges justified their decisions by appealing to the legislative scheme, which was based on the premise that all medical treatment requires consent given by or on behalf of the patient. The Act established a scheme for consent to be given on behalf of patients who were incapable of giving consent. This substituted consent was to be given in accordance with the patients' wishes or (if none) their best interests. The Act also established a process for resolving disputes about patient wishes and best interests.

Although the majority and dissenting judges agreed that this was the scheme of the Act, they drew opposite conclusions about whether it applied to the withdrawal of treatment. The majority concluded that references to withdrawal of treatment in provisions dealing with a "plan of treatment" demonstrated that the scheme was intended to cover withdrawal of treatment generally.[18] The dissenting judges concluded that the reference to withdrawal of treatment in a "plan of treatment" demonstrated that it was not a form of "treatment" to which the Act applied.[19]

As *Cuthberston v Rasouli* demonstrates, it is not always easy to infer the purposes of legislation and there can be disagreement about what purposes are to be inferred. This is particularly true of legislation framed in very general terms, often affording broad discretion to those who administer it. This is why it can be useful to expressly state the purposes in legislation.

Purpose statements have become more common in recent years, particularly in legislation having broad social significance, such as legislation for the protection of human rights or the environment.[20] The increasing use of purpose statements also has a political source in terms of communicating messages to the public about the benefits the legislation seeks to achieve (although whether it actually achieves them will not become clear until many years later).

The most basic form of purpose statement is the title attached to the legislation. The conventional form of the long title for bills in Canada begins with "An Act to." Depending on what follows, the purposes may or may not be clear. For example, a title such as "An Act to amend the Criminal Code" says little about its purposes apart from indicating they have something to do with the *Criminal Code*.

Purposes may be stated in the body of the legislation as one of its numbered sections ("purpose clauses") or they may be stated in preambles preceding the clause giving legislative force to these sections (the "enacting clause"). There is little difference between the interpretive effect of purposes stated either way since Interpretation and Legislation Acts generally provide that preambles are to be "read as part of the enactment intended to assist in explaining its purport and object."[21] The difference between preambles and purpose clauses is mainly one of perspective. Preambles (as the name suggests) look backward ("pre") and explain what has led to the enactment of legislation; purpose clauses are forward-looking, outlining what the legislation is intended to achieve. However, in so far as purposes are often framed in terms of reasons for enactment, they fit into either preambles (explaining what has prompted the legislation) or purpose clauses (explaining what the legislation is to do to address the reasons for making it).

Finally, purposes may be stated in provisions conferring power to do things, like make regulations. Regulation-making provisions are frequently drafted in the form of "X may make regulations *for the purpose of*," however, these clauses often simply refer to "the purposes of this Act," which provides little insight into the purposes, although it underscores a fundamental requirement of regulation-making generally that it conform to the purposes of the enabling Act.

Purposes may also be inferred from a variety of contextual elements such as events leading up to the enactment of legislation (including prior legislation and parliamentary debates) and related international law instruments.[22] These and other contextual elements are considered next.

CHAPTER EIGHT

Context

When people speak to each other, they often share a common understanding about the subject of their conversation. This allows them to speak in an elliptical manner without having to state some of the details of the subject matter they are discussing. They can also clarify their understanding with questions and comments.

Legislation is more limited in terms of the context that can be relied on when conveying meaning. It also involves a much more formally constrained form of communication between one group of people (legislators) and another (those to whom the legislation applies). Achieving a shared understanding among so many people is more challenging. There is also no opportunity for those affected by the legislation to ask legislators questions to clarify the meaning. As noted above, legislators have no role in the application of legislation. It must speak for itself. But it nevertheless speaks within certain contextual features that play an important role in understanding and applying it.

Several types of context have a bearing on the interpretation of legislation. This section considers them under the following headings:

- Immediate Legislative Context
- Broader Legislative Context

- Other Laws and Legal Principles
- External Context

Immediate Legislative Context

Legislative context consists of things of a legislative nature. It first and foremost includes the words surrounding those being interpreted as well as other provisions of the same legislation and delegated legislation made under it.[1] Some of these provisions make statements about the purposes of the legislation and, as noted above, are relevant to determining what these purposes are. This context is accessible to everyone who has access to the legislative text and is reinforced by the maxim that ignorance of the law is no excuse.

Legislative context includes features (also called components) such as tables of contents, headings, notes, numbering, and punctuation that are published with legislative provisions. They are added to help readers understand and apply the legislation and can be very useful in appreciating the "Act as a whole" (its scheme and structure) and navigating around it to find the provisions that apply to a particular situation. Courts have repeatedly stressed the need to consider this context.[2]

Together, these provisions and features form the basis for drawing textual inferences or determining legislative purposes, as discussed above. For example, tautology can arise only when another provision is found to say the same thing as the one being interpreted. By the same token, headings and notes are often framed in terms of purposes.

Although these provisions and features influence the interpretation and application of legislation, they do not all have the same influence. The provisions of the legislation (including preambles and titles) have the most influence because legislators have deliberated on and enacted them. Other features, such as headings and notes, have historically been added by publishers after the legislation has been enacted. Because they are not "enacted" by the legislators, they have had less influence. Procedural rules have also reinforced this by preventing them from being amended during the enactment process.[3] Their secondary interpretive status is also reinforced by some Interpretation Acts providing, for example, that headings and marginal notes "do not form part of the enactment, but are inserted for convenience only."[4] However, these features now appear in bills from the time they are introduced and are in that sense indistinguishable from the provisions of the legislation. Restrictions on amendment during enactment have also been relaxed.[5] Canadian courts now consider these features as a matter of course and give them whatever weight they consider appropriate.[6]

Broader Legislative Context

The Statute Book

A further layer of legislative context is provided by other legislation enacted by the same legislator. It is often referred to as the "Statute Book," although it typically spans many printed volumes (the Revised Statutes of Canada, 1985 consists of 11 volumes).

Like the immediate legislative context, the broader legislative context provides a basis for drawing the textual inferences discussed above. The drafting principles of consistency and no tautology can also be applied across a statute book produced by a single legislative author. For example, in *Boros v University Hospital Board*, the court had to determine the scope of a provision limiting the civil liability of a hospital or nursing home.[7] It looked at provisions in other legislation similarly protecting other medical institutions, noting that the scope of protection in them was limited by wording not found in the hospital and nursing home provision. It concluded these limits were excluded here by their expression in the other legislation.[8]

Reconciling Conflicting Legislation

The rule of law requires legislative provisions to be consistent with one another. Courts assume legislators are aware of their existing legislation and do not intend to enact legislation that contradicts it without amending it expressly to avoid contradiction or specifying that one provision prevails over another. However, given the breadth of the statute books and the haste that sometimes attends the enactment of legislation, conflicting provisions have occurred from time to time.

Canadian courts have taken a narrow approach to defining conflict (and have coincidentally permitted overlap), seeking to allow legislation to operate as fully as possible. Their approach is outlined in *Thibodeau v Air Canada*:

> [C]ourts find that there is a conflict only when the existence of the conflict, in the restrictive sense of the word, cannot be avoided by interpretation. Overlap, on its own, does not constitute conflict in this context, so that even where the ambit of two provisions overlaps, there is a presumption that they both are meant to apply, provided that they can do so without producing absurd results. This presumption may be rebutted if one of the provisions was intended to cover the subject matter exhaustively. . . . [O]nly where a conflict is unavoidable should the court resort to statutory provisions and principles of interpretation concerned with which law takes precedence over the other.[9]

The restrictive notion of conflict has also been justified in terms of preventing the application of one provision from precluding the application of another.[10]

In *Thibodeau*, the Court found there was no conflict between a provision of the *Official Languages Act*[11] authorizing an "appropriate and just remedy" for a violation of that Act and a provision in an international convention implemented by the *Carriage by Air Act*[12] limiting remedies for aviation accident. The "appropriate and just" language of the *Official Languages Act* was interpreted to accommodate the limits in the convention.

An example of a court finding a conflict is *Schnarr v Blue Mountain Resorts Limited*, where the Ontario Court of Appeal found that authority for occupiers of land (in this case, a ski resort) to obtain waivers of civil liability from entrants (skiers) under the *Occupiers' Liability Act*[13] conflicted with a requirement in the *Consumer Protection Act, 2002*[14] that services be "of reasonably acceptable quality."[15] In resolving the conflict, the court said, "The principles of statutory interpretation urge an approach that allows both statutes to maintain their maximum application and effectiveness."[16] However, the court chose to apply the *Occupiers' Liability Act* on the basis that it had been enacted to codify the law relating to this subject and that it was more specific than the *Consumer Protection Act*.[17] This approach allows both provisions to operate, the more specific provisions effectively being an exception to the more general one. The court reinforced its conclusion with an analysis of the consequences of concluding otherwise, finding that to do so would produce an "absurd" result.[18]

Another approach to resolving conflicts is to apply the provision that was enacted later.[19] This approach turns on the notion of implied repeal: the later enactment impliedly repeals the earlier one.[20] However, courts are generally quite reluctant to apply this approach and do so only if the conflict cannot be resolved in any other way.[21]

Legislation from Other Jurisdictions

The broader legislative context also includes legislation enacted in other jurisdictions, particularly others in Canada. Jurisdictions sometimes look to each other's legislation when determining how to frame their own.[22] *Canada (Canadian Human Rights Commission) v Canada (Attorney General)* provides an example of the influence of legislation from other jurisdictions.[23] It involved a reference to "expenses" in a provision authorizing a human rights tribunal to make orders providing redress for discriminatory conduct. The issue was whether this term included legal costs incurred to bring a complaint. The Supreme Court decided it did not, relying in part on specific references to "costs" in some provincial legislation, but not in the *Canadian Human Rights Act*.[24] Although this feature was not in itself sufficient to support the Court's conclusion, it was in combination with other contextual features (notably enactment proceedings).

Other Laws

Legislation does not operate in a vacuum. It interacts with other forms of law recognized in Canada. It is based on constitutional law, which provides the foundation for all law in Canada. Canadian law is also generally recognized as pluralistic, incorporating different legal systems. Common law, civil law, and international law are well-recognized as fundamental components of Canadian law. More recently, Indigenous legal traditions are being recognized as well. This recognition is being accelerated by the United Nations Declaration on the Rights of Indigenous Peoples and legislation providing for its implementation in Canadian law.[25] An example of Indigenous legal traditions woven into legislation is the *Aboriginal Custom Adoption Recognition Act* of the Northwest Territories and Nunavut.[26]

Constitutional Law

The Constitution is an amalgam of written law (legislation), unwritten law (common law), and conventions (non-binding rules), largely inherited from the United Kingdom or enacted by its Parliament.[27] However, since 1982, any changes to the Constitution must be made by Canadian legislative institutions (the Governor General, Senate and House of Commons, and the provincial lieutenant governors and legislative assemblies) in accordance with Part 5 of the *Constitution Act, 1982*.

There are three main elements of the Constitution affecting the interpretation and application of legislation. One is the *Constitution Act, 1867*,[28] which establishes government institutions and divides legislative powers between the federal Parliament and the provincial legislatures. The second is the *Canadian Charter of Rights and Freedoms*,[29] which protects a variety of rights and freedoms from government action, or requires government action.[30] The third is section 35 of the *Constitution Act, 1982*, which recognizes Aboriginal and treaty rights. Constitutional principles such as the rule of law, legislative sovereignty, democracy, respect for minorities, and the honour of the Crown can also influence the interpretation of legislation.[31]

The Constitution is the supreme law of Canada and prevails over other inconsistent laws.[32] This priority manifests itself in two ways. First, another law that is "inconsistent" with the Constitution "is, to the extent of the inconsistency, of no force or effect." Second, the Constitution can prevail through its effect on the interpretation of legislation, which is presumed to be enacted in accordance with the Constitution.[33] In addition, when legislation is expressed in very general terms, *Charter* values (as opposed to its legal requirements) may be taken into consideration. For example, in *R v Mabior,* the Supreme Court considered the meaning of "fraud" in a provision of the *Criminal Code*[34] dealing with sexual assault. Chief Justice McLachlin said:

> [48] In keeping with the *Charter* values of equality and autonomy, we now see sexual assault not only as a crime associated with emotional and physical harm to the victim, but as the wrongful exploitation of another human being. To engage in sexual acts without the consent of another person is to treat him or her as an object and negate his or her human dignity. Although the *Charter* is not directly engaged, the values that animate it must be taken into account in interpreting s. 265(3)(c) of the *Criminal Code.*[35]

However, the Supreme Court has also held that *Charter* values can only be taken into consideration when the text is ambiguous ("subject to differing, but equally plausible interpretations").[36] Despite the circularity of this argument (given that ambiguity depends on context, which includes the Constitution), the Supreme Court has continued to reiterate this threshold for considering *Charter* values.[37]

Indigenous Rights and Legal Traditions

Indigenous rights and legal traditions have existed since long before the arrival of Europeans in the Americas.[38] Many of them, such as the traditions of the Haudenasonee Confederacy,[39] rivalled European governance systems in their development and arguably formed the basis for federalist institutions later adopted in the United States.[40]

Canadian courts have recognized that these rights and traditions survived the assertion of sovereignty by the colonial powers and were absorbed into the common law.[41] They have also been recognized in treaties, particularly modern treaties dealing with self-government.[42] With the constitutional recognition of existing Aboriginal and Treaty rights in section 35 of the *Constitution Act, 1982*, these traditions are now constitutionally protected. However, the impact of these rights and legal traditions on the interpretation of legislation has been doubtful. Although the Supreme Court of Canada has said treaties and statutes relating to Indigenous peoples "should be liberally construed and doubtful expressions resolved in favour of the [Indigenous peoples],"[43] it has declined to apply the treaty approach of interpreting the legislation as Indigenous peoples would have understood it.[44] And, as concerns legislation that applies generally, the courts have been even less inclined to adopt an Indigenous perspective. For example, in *Council of the Wasauksing First Nation v Wausasink Lands Inc*, the Ontario Court of Appeal refused to give effect to First Nations customs and practices in an application for the rectification of corporate records under the *Corporations Act*.[45]

The enactment of legislation for the implementation of the UN Declaration on the Rights of Indigenous Peoples provides an opportunity for greater recognition of Indigenous rights and legal traditions, particularly in implementing legislation.[46] However, it remains to be seen how this implementation will be carried out and how long it will take.

Common Law

As noted above,[47] the common law originated in England and is expressed in court decisions dealing with a wide variety of matters. Some are matters of "public law" dealing with governmental bodies and their relationships with private individuals and corporations. Others are a matter of "private law" dealing with relationships between private individuals and corporations. The public law aspects of the common law apply throughout Canada (including Quebec); the private law aspects apply in all provinces and territories except Quebec.

The constitutional principle of legislative sovereignty recognizes that Parliament and the provincial and territorial legislatures can change the common law or replace it with legislative provisions. However, legislation does not necessarily do this. It can instead incorporate concepts and rules from the common law. For example, the *Criminal Code* incorporates common law defences.[48] It also contains many offences relating to property (theft, breaking and entering, false pretenses), but it does not say what property is.[49] It relies on common law and civil law (for application in Quebec) to define property and the related concept of ownership.

Legislation can also supplement the common law with additional rules or restate it in a codified form (without altering it). One of the principal purposes of a "code" is to consolidate existing law, as was done in the late nineteenth century when Canada first enacted its *Criminal Code*.[50]

How legislation relates to the common law depends on its interpretation. Courts have traditionally been quite protective of the common law, requiring any changes to it, or indeed its abrogation, to be very clearly expressed.[51] This protectiveness is rooted in a concern for the stability of the law and an assumption that legislators are aware of the common law and can clearly express their intent to change it if they so desire.[52] Courts have recognized that provisions such as the following from the Ontario *Occupiers' Liability Act* are capable of doing this:

> **Common law duty of care superseded**
> 2. Subject to section 9, **this Act applies in place of the rules of the common law** that determine the care that the occupier of premises at common law is required to show for the purpose of determining the occupier's liability in law in respect of dangers to persons entering on the premises or the property brought on the premises by those persons.[53]

Courts more readily find that legislation incorporates the common law[54] or that it simply adds to the common law without altering it.[55]

Civil Law

Private law matters in Quebec are governed by its *Civil Code*,[56] which operates within a civil law system originating in Roman law. The *Civil Code* is legislation enacted by the legislature of Quebec, which has the authority to change it like other legislation. However, the *Civil Code*, much like the common law, constitutes an important foundation for the operation of other legislation dealing with private law matters and generally supplements that legislation.[57]

Multijural Legislation

The common law and civil law operate alternatively depending on whether legislation applies in Quebec or elsewhere in Canada. This means federal legislation (which operates throughout Canada) must be capable of operating in conjunction with civil law in Quebec and common law elsewhere. This is known as "bijuralism" and is achieved by drafting federal legislation to connect with both legal systems. The drafting techniques used to do this are:

1. Using both common law and civil law terminology ("doubles");[58] or
2. Using neutral or generic terms that speak to both legal systems.[59]

The use of the first technique is recognized in section 8.2 of the federal *Interpretation Act*:

> **Terminology**
> **8.2** Unless otherwise provided by law, when an enactment contains both civil law and common law terminology, or terminology that has a different meaning in the civil law and the common law, the civil law terminology or meaning is to be adopted in the Province of Quebec and the common law terminology or meaning is to be adopted in the other provinces.[60]

With the burgeoning recognition of Indigenous legal traditions, it is also possible another form of multijural legislation may apply these traditions as alternatives to rules that apply to non-Indigenous people. There are already examples of legislation providing rules for Indigenous peoples, some of which incorporate their legal traditions such as those relating to adoption.[61]

International Law

International law governs nation-states. However, it can be received into Canadian law in two ways.

First, customary international law is considered part of the common law and applies to the extent that it is not inconsistent with other Canadian law, including legislation.[62] However, it constitutes a relatively small portion of international law that must be widely recognized internationally through general practice and belief that the practice amounts to a legal obligation.[63]

The second way relates to international obligations resulting from treaties, conventions, or other agreements between or among nation-states. In Canada, these obligations do not constitute part of Canadian law unless legislation has been enacted to implement them. Implementation can be accomplished using either or both of two techniques. The first is to incorporate the agreement into Canadian law. The simplest way to do this is to provide that it has "the force of law."[64] In these cases, the terms of the agreement are interpreted in accordance with international law principles stated in the Vienna Convention on the Law of Treaties.[65] The second technique involves the enactment of legislation stating the substance of the obligations contemplated by the agreement.[66]

Although international agreements have no direct legal effect without implementing legislation, they can influence the interpretation of legislation when the legislation is ambiguous (two different possible interpretations).[67] The courts presume legislators prefer interpretations that accord with international agreements. The "values and principles" they express can also influence interpretation in these situations, prompting courts to adopt the interpretation that best reflects them.[68] This approach is similar to that taken to *Charter* values in that it requires ambiguity.[69]

Legal Policy Presumptions

The laws discussed above are not the only legal matters contributing to the context for interpreting legislation. The courts have also developed a series of interpretive presumptions expressing views about how the legal system should operate (legal policies). The main ones have traditionally been:

- Reserving the criminal justice system for clearly defined and seriously injurious or disruptive behaviour[70]
- Restricting taxation to clearly defined activities that taxpayers can plan for and arrange so as to minimize the tax they must pay[71]
- Protecting proprietary rights and contractual freedom[72]
- Upholding due process and fairness in government decision-making[73]
- Protecting the role of lawyers and the jurisdiction of courts and tribunals in ensuring the rule of law[74]

These legal policies have generally been advanced through the strict interpretation of legislation, requiring very clear legislative language to infringe these policies.

More recently the courts have also recognized legal policies related to:

- The protection of fundamental human rights and Indigenous rights
- Entitlement to social benefits[75]

These policies are advanced through a liberal (generous) interpretation of the rights and benefit provisions in favour of those claiming them. However, Canadian courts have more recently qualified the scope for strict or liberal interpretation by limiting their application to cases where ambiguity remains after the text and purposes of the legislation have been considered.[76]

External Context

The discussion of context up to this point has focused on legal matters — legislation and other forms of law related to the provisions being interpreted. External context consists of circumstances and events surrounding the enactment of legislation that do not constitute law, including:

- The social and historical context in which the legislation was enacted
- The proceedings resulting in the enactment of the legislation
- Previously enacted legislation that has been amended or replaced by the legislation being interpreted
- Legislative models produced by law reform bodies

Social and Historical Context

Circumstances and events leading up to the enactment of legislation can help in understanding what the legislation is intended to deal with and its purposes in doing so. Sometimes courts take judicial notice of this context[77] or consider it as a matter of common sense[78] and have been increasingly receptive to scientific or historical evidence.[79]

Legislative Evolution

Legislative evolution has to do with how legislators change the text of legislative provisions over time and "consists of the provision's initial formulation and all subsequent formulations."[80]

Legislation is sometimes changed to improve its readability or correct minor errors.[81] The best examples of this are the statute revisions that have been enacted periodically throughout Canada.[82]

However, changes to legislation are more often substantive. Comparing the current and previous versions may reveal the nature of these changes and provide a basis for inferring their underlying purposes. For example, in *Crupi v Canada Employment and Immigration Commission*, the wording of a provision limiting employment insurance benefits was shortened from an inmate of "any prison or penitentiary or an institution supported wholly or partly out of public funds" to "any prison or similar institution."[83] The change was interpreted to indicate an intention to exclude non-penal institutions such as hospitals.[84]

Legislative evolution also includes proposed changes that were not made.[85] If the legislature declines to enact a change, it suggests the provision has a meaning that does not include what was proposed as a change. For example, in *Canada (Canadian Human Rights Commission) v Canada (Attorney General)*, bills had been introduced to amend a provision authorizing a human rights tribunal to order the payment of "expenses" incurred by a complainant found to have been subject to discriminatory conduct.[86] Amendments had been proposed to the *Canadian Human Rights Act*[87] to add a reference to legal "costs," but the amendments were not passed. The Supreme Court relied on this (as well as other factors) to conclude that "expenses" did not extend to "costs." However, it also cautioned that "great care must be taken in deciding how much, if any, weight to give to these sorts of material."[88] This caution reflects the fact that, as noted above, changes are sometimes made to clarify or resolve doubts about the scope of a legislative provision rather than change its substance.

Legislative Proceedings (History)

When interpreting and applying legislation, Canadian courts are prepared to consider proceedings relating to its enactment, often referred to as "legislative history." These proceedings include transcripts of debates (*Hansard*), evidence presented to legislative committees, and the reports of these committees. However, in *Re Rizzo &*

Rizzo Shoes Ltd, the Supreme Court qualified the significance of these proceedings, saying, "Although the frailties of Hansard evidence are many, this Court has recognized that it can play a limited role in the interpretation of legislation."[89] The "frailties" of *Hansard* and other materials relating to legislative proceedings result from the political partisanship or self-interest of many of those who participate in these proceedings and the fact that their views are not necessarily shared widely among the legislators involved.[90] For example, a minister may be presumed to speak on behalf of all government members; it is less clear on whose behalf a backbench member is speaking.

The courts have most often used legislative proceedings to establish the purposes of legislation.[91] More recently, the Supreme Court has taken up Ruth Sullivan's suggestion that they can also be used to establish the meaning of the text if they are reliable.[92] However, given the volume of legislation enacted and the relatively limited time for debate, it is rare that legislative proceedings address the meaning of specific words that end up being subject to interpretation.

Reports and Legislative Models

Legislation is often enacted after studies have been conducted of policy matters requiring legislation. These studies may be conducted by governmental bodies or by others, for example, law reform commissions, having some independence from government. These studies also sometimes include recommendations in the form of draft legislation. For example, in Ontario the *Occupiers' Liability Act*[93] was enacted based on a report of the Law Reform Commission of Ontario.[94] By the same token, for more than 100 years a federal-provincial-territorial body, the Uniform Law Conference of Canada, has developed model legislation on a wide variety of topics to achieve legislative uniformity across Canada's provincial and territorial jurisdictions. Many of its model Acts have been enacted in jurisdictions across Canada, resulting in substantial uniformity across the country.[95]

Canadian courts will consider these reports and legislative models when interpreting and applying legislation relating to them. For example, in *Sound Stage Entertainment Inc v Burns*, the Saskatchewan Court of Appeal considered section 3 of *The Contributory Negligence Act*,[96] which provided for the apportionment of damages caused by the "fault" of two or more persons. The court had to decide whether "fault" included libelous or other intentional acts.[97] The court decided it did not, basing its conclusion on its understanding of the objects of the Act as suggested by its legislative history, including the work of the Uniform Law Conference, which formed the basis for the enactment of the Act. This work involved a series of drafts and commentary, which vacillated between using "fault" and "negligence," with "fault" in the final version of the model Act. From this, the court concluded "In the end, therefore, the work of the Uniform Law Conference rather strongly suggests that the word 'fault,' at least as it is used in s. 3 of the *Act*, refers only to negligence."[98]

Other Interpreters

To ensure legislation is interpreted to have a single meaning, a judge may take notice of how other judges have interpreted the legislation and interpret it in accordance with previous decisions. In addition, the doctrine of precedent requires lower courts to adhere to interpretations of higher courts, which resolve conflicting interpretations of lower courts. However, it is sometimes debatable whether a previous decision is a binding precedent or can instead be distinguished as dealing with a different situation.[99] And although judges are not bound by decisions made by other judges of the same court, they will give them due consideration and not lightly depart from them.[100]

Appellate courts can overrule their previous decisions, but they do not do so lightly. This occurs only in very limited circumstances involving new legal issues resulting from significant developments in the law or fundamental changes of circumstances or evidence.[101]

Court decisions on the interpretation of legislation in another jurisdiction do not engage the doctrine of precedent, but courts often consider them and will follow them if they find their reasoning persuasive and applicable in cases before them.[102]

Although courts are the ultimate interpreters of legislation, they are not the only ones. And since the late twentieth century, Canadian courts have increasingly acknowledged that some non-judicial interpreters are entitled to deference when it comes to understanding and applying legislation. The Supreme Court's decision in *Canada v Vavilov* makes the point in confirming that interpretations by administrative bodies (for example, human rights tribunals) are generally to be reviewed on the standard of reasonableness, which recognizes there may be a range of "reasonable" interpretations, as opposed to only one "correct" interpretation.[103] When applying the reasonableness standard, courts will not interfere with a "reasonable" interpretation, even though they might consider another interpretation to be "correct." This is consistent with the Court's recognition that interpretations reflected in administrative practice[104] as well as delegated legislation[105] and quasi-legislation (such as policies and guidelines)[106] are also entitled to consideration when courts determine interpretive questions.

CHAPTER NINE

Application

Understanding what legislation means in general does not itself answer the question of how it applies in a particular fact situation. Legislation is seldom interpreted in the abstract. People read it to resolve practical questions arising in particular circumstances. The attention of courts is overwhelmingly focused on resolving these questions. And application provisions do not resolve all questions about how legislation applies in particular circumstances; application provisions often themselves require interpretation to understand how they apply.

The meaning attributed to a legislative text is influenced by the facts to which it is being applied. This is clearly demonstrated by the way Canadian courts use the concept of plausibility and consider the consequences of applying an interpretation to particular facts (consequential analysis). This chapter begins by considering how they do this.

Legislation sometimes contains application provisions describing what its other provisions apply to. Application provisions are typically found at the beginning of legislation along with definitions and other interpretive provisions, which also inform the application of the rest of the legislation.

Application provisions can also be found within particular provisions. Many provisions contain "cases" or conditions consisting of subordinate clauses beginning with "if," "when," or "where." These too constitute application provisions describing the circumstances in which the provision operates (or does not).

Application provisions are as vast and variable as the subject matter of legislation itself. However, three aspects of application deserve particular attention because of how often they arise in the interpretation and application of legislation:

- time
- territory
- the state

This chapter (and indeed this book) concludes by considering these aspects and the types of provisions typically used to address them.

Plausibility

Canadian courts frequently say the meaning of a legislative text must be plausible. Plausibility is related to the ordinary or technical meaning associated with words. This meaning is used to determine whether the words apply in particular circumstances.[1] For example, in *Godbout v Pagé*, the issue was whether the words "suffered . . . in an accident" applied to injuries occurring after an automobile accident as a result of negligent medical treatment.[2] The Court decided these words plausibly applied, concluding "[the injury] originated in a series of events that have a plausible, logical and sufficiently close link to one another and have, in each case, the automobile accident as their starting point."[3]

Plausibility limits the scope for applying the text to matters it encompasses and sometimes operates in opposition to the purposes of the legislation. Tension between the text and the purposes is one of the most pervasive and difficult aspects of understanding and applying legislation. It is about balancing access to the law (afforded by the text) and respect for the legislator's primary role in making law (purposes). Plausibility recognizes that legislative purposes must find expression in the text.[4] And if the text does not express those purposes, they have no legal force.

Although plausibility reinforces the role of the text in understanding and applying legislation, it sometimes gives way to purposive considerations, particularly when they are supported by contextual elements. Just as some things are left unsaid in ordinary discourse, so too courts are occasionally prepared to "read in" additional words, particularly to limit the scope of a provision. For example, in *Re Vabalis* the court limited the application of a spousal consent requirement for a name-change application to spouses with the same last name.[5] This result reflected the substantial decline in married women assuming the last names of their husbands. Similarly, in *Felipa v Canada (Citizenship and Immigration)*, the court added an age limit to a provision authorizing superior court judges to act as judges of the Federal Court.[6] This limit reflected the age limit the *Federal Courts Act*[7] imposed on the appointment of judges to the court.

Courts also sometimes find ancillary powers are conferred by necessary implication to support the exercise of expressly conferred powers.[8] In these cases, practical considerations arising from the application of provisions conferring these powers provide substantial contextual support for implying the additional powers.

To some extent, these reading-in cases involve courts doing the work of legislators, updating legislation, or adding important details. However, courts also frequently decline to do this work and leave it to legislators to decide whether to amend their legislation.[9] Much depends on how substantial a court considers the updating or additional details to be. Are they relatively minor or do they deserve the legislator's attention?

Consequential Analysis

Canadian courts consider the results of applying a legislative text in the circumstances before them. Their consideration of results is often framed in terms of whether the results are "absurd." Legislators are presumed not to intend such results.

Although "absurdity" is open-ended and prone to subjective assessment, courts have narrowed it to particular types of matters.[10] Legislators are presumed not to intend results that

- involve unreasonable distinctions[11]
- are too impractical to enforce[12]
- defeat statutory purpose(s)[13]
- contradict "common sense"[14]
- deal with trivial matters[15]

There is debate about using consequential analysis to resolve competing interpretations of legislation.[16] Debate arises when it is difficult to find a plausible interpretation (based on the ordinary or technical meaning of the text) that avoids an absurd result. This is similar to the tension noted above in the discussion of plausibility between the text and the purposes of the legislation. In these cases, there is seldom a clear answer. The best that can be said is as Sullivan suggests:

> The greater the absurdity to be avoided, the further the court may stray from the constraints of the text; conversely, the clearer the provision and the plainer its meaning, the greater the absurdity required to justify departure from the text.[17]

Application in Time

Time influences the application of legislation in two different ways.

First, the meaning and usage of words change over time. Natural languages such as English and French constantly evolve with changing social conditions and new inventions and technologies. For example, the word "alien" in the nineteenth century meant someone from another country. Although it retains this meaning today, its dominant meaning now is a being from another planet.

Second, the application of legislation depends on when the relevant facts happened. It does not generally apply to events happening before it is made (retroactivity) or after it is repealed. It also often does not apply in relation to things that existed before it was made (retrospectivity).

These two aspects are discussed next in terms of *Original and Current Meaning* and *Prospectivity, Retroactivity, and Retrospectivity.*

Original and Current Meaning

A fundamental purpose of legislation is to provide a legal mechanism for law-makers to realize their policy objectives. Its meaning must give effect to those objectives. But natural languages such as English and French evolve over time. The meaning and usage of words change. With older legislation, there may be questions about what meaning is to be given some words.

In these cases, courts apply the meaning at the time the legislation was enacted. This reflects the intention of those who made it since they are assumed to have used words in the sense current at that time. However, this approach does not necessarily reflect the goal of legislation to communicate effectively to those it affects. If an original meaning is no longer current, people in the present day may be misled into applying a current meaning that differs from the previous ("original") one. Nevertheless, courts have in this regard prioritized the intent of the law-maker over intelligibility to the public.

An authoritative example is *R v Perka* involving a reference to "*cannabis sativa L.*" in the *Narcotic Control Act*.[18] The Supreme Court gave this term the quite broad meaning it had when it was enacted, as opposed to the narrower meaning it acquired later as scientific and general interest in this substance increased in the 1960s.[19] The Court particularly noted the application of original meaning to technical terms (like the botanical one in question here):

> [W]here, as here, the legislature has deliberately chosen a specific scientific or technical term to represent an equally specific and particular class of things, it would do violence to Parliament's intent to give a new meaning to that term whenever the taxonomic

> consensus among members of the relevant scientific fraternity shifted. It is clear that Parliament intended in 1961, by the phrase "*Cannabis sativa* L.", to prohibit all cannabis.[20]

The application of original meaning may be more expansive when words have broader meaning. The fact that they would have been interpreted narrowly when the legislation was made does not necessarily mean they are to be given such an interpretation when they are applied in the present. The best-known example of this is the so-called Persons Case involving the appointment of senators under section 24 of the *Constitution Act, 1867*.[21] This section authorized the Governor General to "summon qualified Persons to the Senate." The Supreme Court of Canada interpreted "Persons" to include only men because, in 1867 (when the Act was passed), the participation of women in public affairs (including voting) was very limited. The Judicial Committee of the Privy Council reversed this decision, noting not only the many textual indications in the Act suggesting "persons" included women, but also that the Act "planted in Canada a living tree capable of growth and expansion within its natural limits."[22] This case is now recognized as the foundation for a dynamic approach to interpreting the laws of the Constitution.[23]

This approach has also been followed in cases interpreting non-constitutional legislation. In *R v Stucky*, the Ontario Court of Appeal approved the following description of when a dynamic approach should be adopted:

> [L]egislation that is enacted to regulate an ongoing activity over an indefinite period of time invites a dynamic interpretation whereas legislation that is aimed at a particular set of circumstances or is otherwise tied to a specific time or place invites a fixed interpretation.[24]

The court had to decide whether the prohibition of false or misleading representations in section 52 of the *Competition Act*[25] could apply to representations made outside Canada. It interpreted "to the public" as including the people outside Canada, even though at the time of enactment the prohibition would have had little application to these people because of Canada's limited role as an exporter.

Courts have also been prepared to apply general terminology to include things that might not have existed when the legislation was made.[26] For example, in *Woods (Re)*, the court interpreted a provision conferring a right to be "present" during a hearing to encompass presence through videoconference technology, even though it did not exist when the provision was enacted.[27]

Coming into Force

The enactment of legislation occurs at the end of a legislative process. In the case of Acts, this process ends with royal assent. At this point, a proposed legislative text becomes a law. But it does not necessarily have the force of law. This is analogous to electrical wiring. Installing the wiring does not itself turn on the lights. A switch must be flicked as well. And so, enacted legislation must also "come into force" to operate as law.

Acts sometimes come into force at the same time as their enactment, but not always. Historically, they did not come into force until the end of the session in which they were enacted.[28] However, most Interpretation Acts now provide that an Act comes into force at the beginning of the day it receives royal assent,[29] but circumstances often make this impractical. For example, a complex piece of legislation may require extensive administrative arrangements to be made before the legislation can function. In these cases, time is needed after royal assent to accomplish this. This is why the Interpretation Act rule of commencement on royal assent can (like other Interpretation Act provisions) be set aside by a "contrary intention" in another provision. This is typically done through "commencement provisions," which enact different dates or times for legislation to come into force.

The *Economic Action Plan Act, No 1* (assented to on 26 June 2013) exemplifies this. It contains a series of commencement provisions establishing commencement dates other than royal assent:

> **Coming into Force**
>
> April 1, 2013
>
> 103. Sections 64 to 102 are deemed to have come into force on April 1, 2013.
>
> . . .
>
> **Coming into Force**
>
> Order in council
>
> 212. Section 211 comes into force on a day to be fixed by order of the Governor in Council.
>
> . . .
>
> **Coming into Force**
>
> Order in council
>
> 232. Subsection 228(2) comes into force, in accordance with subsection 114(4) of the *Canada Pension Plan*, on a day to be fixed by order of the Governor in Council.[30]

The first of these examples (section 103) brings the specified provisions into force retroactively, before the legislation was enacted. This is typically done for taxation legislation; the commencement is retroactive to the date of the Budget Speech announcing the legislation.

The second example (section 212) is most frequently used. It delegates power to the Executive (the Governor General acting on the advice of the Cabinet) to set the date. A comparable (and generally applicable) provision is section 8(3) of the Ontario *Legislation Act, 2006*, which delegates this power to the Lieutenant Governor in Council. These provisions also allow different dates to be set for different provisions. Although this gives the Executive considerable discretion to bring some provisions into force but not others, Canadian courts have not questioned this.[31] However, concerns have been expressed about the Executive's failure to bring provisions into force and some jurisdictions have enacted legislation to provide for the repeal of provisions that have not been brought into force after a lengthy period (typically at least ten years).[32]

The third example (section 232) requires the consent of lieutenant governors in council of two-thirds of provinces with two-thirds of the Canadian population before the commencement order can be made. It is very unusual, but reflects the federal-provincial dimensions of the legislation it relates to (*Canada Pension Plan*).[33]

The coming into force of delegated legislation is usually governed by Acts dealing with processes for making this legislation, such as the federal *Statutory Instruments Act*,[34] the Ontario *Legislation Act, 2006*,[35] and the Quebec *Regulations Act*.[36] These Acts provide that government regulations generally come into force when they are filed or registered under them, or after they have been published in an official gazette. They also limit the legal effectiveness of regulations before their publication.[37]

Prospectivity, Retroactivity, and Retrospectivity

The constitutional principle of the rule of law requires that people have fair notice of, and access to, laws that apply to them.[38] This principle provides a basis for people to respect and rely on the law. Legislation should apply to matters arising after it comes into force so that those affected by it can be aware of the legislation and arrange their affairs accordingly at that time. This is known as "prospective" application.

If a law applies to what people do before it is in force, they could not have known with certainty that it would have legal effect at that time. These situations are generally characterized as involving "retroactive" or "retrospective" application. Although the rule of law militates against this, another constitutional principle, parliamentary sovereignty, recognizes that primary legislative bodies (Parliament and the provincial and territorial legislatures) can enact legislation that applies to matters in the past, subject to two exceptions recognized in the *Canadian Charter of Rights and Freedoms*: they cannot make offences apply to conduct occurring before they are in force and they cannot deny a person the benefit of a lesser punishment that was in effect when they committed an offence.[39]

The authority of primary legislative bodies to enact legislation applying to matters in the past is counterbalanced by an interpretive presumption that these bodies do not intend to do so unless they make that intention very clear.[40] The strength of this presumption depends on the degree to which the legislation imposes adverse consequences on those affected by it. The severity of these consequences is often characterized in terms of interference with "vested rights," which have a "tangible and concrete" quality, are not subject to any contingency, and have begun to deliver ("accrue") benefits to the holders of the rights.[41] The presumption is also reinforced by transitional provisions in Interpretation Acts outlining matters that are not affected by the repeal or replacement of legislative provisions, unless a contrary intention is expressed.[42] These matters include a right or obligation to do something in the past and penal liability for doing things in the past that were prohibited when they were done. An intention to affect these matters must be clearly expressed, as it has been in transitional provisions in amending legislation. For example, Parliament enacted section 5.1(4) of the *Department of Veterans Affairs Act* in 1990:

> (4) No claim shall be made after this subsection comes into force for or on account of interest on moneys held or administered by the Minister during any period prior to January 1, 1990 pursuant to *subsection 41(1)* of the *Pension Act*, subsection 15(2) of the *War Veterans Allowance Act* or any regulations made under section 5 of this Act.[43]

The severity of consequences also depends on the scope of interference, which can be differentiated into two categories. One involves applying legislation as if it had been in force in the past ("retroactivity"). The other involves applying legislation prospectively to matters that arose in the past ("retrospectivity"). This distinction can also be illustrated by legislation adding a term to contracts made before it comes into force. If it adds the term so that it applies as of some time before the legislation comes into force, the legislation is *retroactive.* If it adds the term, but makes it apply only after the legislation is in force, it is *retrospective.*[44]

Retroactivity generally entails more serious interference with what people have done in the past, and the presumption against it is difficult to rebut without express language. Perhaps the clearest way to do this is to provide that legislation "is deemed to have come into force" on a date in the past.[45] Another is a provision "declaring" the meaning of previously enacted legislation.[46]

Retrospectivity is a generally less serious interference, and courts are more receptive to it when it benefits those to whom it applies, has a general public benefit,[47] or deals with matters of procedure.[48] In other circumstances, the presumption can be overcome when retrospective effect "is expressly or is expressly or by necessary implication required by the language of the Act."[49]

Territorial Application

Legislation is generally presumed to apply throughout the territory of the body that enacts it,[50] but legislators can provide that legislation has effect only in particular localities, for example, legislation establishing municipal governments.[51]

Legislation is also presumed to apply only within the territory of the enacting legislature.[52] This presumption is based on respect for the territorial sovereignty of other jurisdictions (which is also a principle of international law)[53] and avoiding conflicting legislation. In the case of provincial legislatures, this presumption is reinforced by section 92 of the *Constitution Act, 1867*, which limits their legislative authority to matters "in the Province."[54] However, some matters involve a combination of elements, some of which are within the territory of the enacting jurisdiction and some of which are outside. Examples are matters of child custody and support when parents have separated and are living in different jurisdictions. In these cases, a substantial connection to the enacting jurisdiction will justify the application of its legislation, for example, the residence of one parent in that jurisdiction.[55]

The federal Parliament is generally recognized to be able to enact legislation that applies outside Canada, although this can raise concerns about intrusion on the sovereignty of other countries. These concerns are the basis for the presumption against extraterritorial application, which can be overcome by clear legislative provisions.[56] Examples of federal legislation having extraterritorial effect are Acts dealing with activities that typically cross international borders, such as aviation and shipping.[57] These Acts are usually enacted in accordance with international agreements addressing international law concerns that would otherwise arise. Parliament has also enacted the *Oceans Act*, which extends Canadian law into waters surrounding Canada that are not within any province or territory.[58]

Application to State Entities

Legislation has not historically applied to the Crown (the king or queen) as the embodiment of the state (including state entities representing the Crown) because the king or queen made the law and it was presumed that, in giving assent to an Act, they intended only to make law for their subjects and not limit their own rights and privileges.[59] This historical notion has been transformed into a presumption now expressed in most Interpretation Acts, which in Canada refer to the Crown as "Her Majesty" or "His Majesty." For example, section 17 of the federal *Interpretation Act* says:

> **Her Majesty not bound or affected unless stated**
> **17.** No enactment is binding on Her Majesty or affects Her Majesty or Her Majesty's rights or prerogatives in any manner, except as mentioned or referred to in the enactment.[60]

This presumption is questionable in modern times when state entities engage in many activities regulated by legislation. In fact, much regulatory legislation, for example, concerning environmental protection, now applies to the Crown by virtue of provisions saying the legislation "is binding on Her Majesty."[61]

British Columbia and Prince Edward Island have dispensed with this presumption in their interpretation legislation.[62] Canadian courts have also demonstrated reservations about applying it. They have recognized not only that it may be overcome by express provisions to the contrary, but also that the Crown may be bound by "logical or necessary implication"[63] or when it accepts the benefits of the legislation.[64] In the twenty-first century, there seems little justification for the presumption of Crown immunity. Two jurisdictions have abolished it without any obvious adverse consequences. It is time for others to follow suit.

ANNEX 1

The Uniform Law Conference of Canada Drafting Conventions

Report of the Committee Appointed to Prepare Bilingual Legislative Drafting Conventions for the Uniform Law Conference of Canada (Majority Report)[1]

Adapted 12–13 August 1989

Introduction

The history of the Canadian Legislative Drafting Conventions and the history of the Uniform Law Conferences are so intertwined as to be virtually inseparable. At its first annual meeting in 1918, the Conference of Commissioners on Uniformity of Laws throughout Canada (as the Uniform Law Conference was then known) appointed a committee to prepare a set of rules for legislative drafting for the Conference. The committee's report was adopted at the second annual meeting in 1919.

In 1941, a committee consisting of Erich H. Silk of Ontario and J.P. Runciman of Saskatchewan was appointed to revise the 1919 rules. This committee's report was received and adopted in 1942. In 1947, the Saskatchewan Commissioners were asked to revise the rules once again. The report of E.C. Leslie and J.P. Runciman was adopted in 1948. The revised rules were included in a pamphlet that was published by the Conference in 1949 under the title Uniformity of Legislation in Canada — An Outline.

The current conventions and commentaries grew out of the work of the Legislative Drafting Workshop (the forerunner of the Legislative Drafting Section), which first met in 1969. After several years of intensive work, particularly on the part of Glen Acorn of Alberta, the present drafting conventions were adopted in 1976. Arthur Norman Stone of Ontario and James Ryan of Newfoundland were appointed to prepare the commentaries. Their report was adopted in 1978. (The 1976 Conventions have been amended twice, in 1981 and 1986.)

The current conventions, like all their predecessors, were adopted in English only and applied only to English drafting. When the Conference began to adopt its uniform legislation in both French and English, official drafting conventions applicable to both languages became necessary. Among others, Gérard Bertrand, Claude Bisaillon, Alain-François Bisson, Alexandre Covacs, Bruno Lalonde, Bernard Méchin and Louis-Philippe Pigeon devoted time to the issue. A draft French document was presented to the annual meeting in 1984, but was not adopted.

By 1987 it was clear that it was neither practical nor realistic to have separate drafting conventions for French drafting and English drafting, each devoting no attention to the rules applicable to the other official language. Consequently, the annual meeting in Winnipeg appointed a committee to prepare bilingual drafting conventions. This committee was to report in 1988, but soon realized that such a major task could not be completed in one year.

The proposed drafting conventions and commentaries set out in this report are based both on the draft French document mentioned above and on the Conference's existing English drafting conventions and commentaries. The members of the committee are grateful for the invaluable work of their predecessors.

The conventions set out in this report were prepared primarily by Cornelia Schuh, Donald Revell and Michel Moisan, all of the Office of the Legislative Counsel in Ontario with significant input from Peter Pagano of Alberta, Michel Nantel of Manitoba,

Gerard. Bertrand and Lionel Levert of Ottawa, Jean Allaire of Quebec and Elaine Doleman and Bruno Lalonde of New Brunswick. Mr. Lalonde's minority report, which is published separately in the 1989 proceedings of the Conference, reminds us that there is more than one approach to the complex subject of legislative drafting.

The Drafting Section of the Conference is a useful forum for the discussion of issues of interest to people who draft in English; it should now perform the same function for those who work in French-speaking and bilingual settings. It is the hope of the authors of this document that the Conference's work in the area of bilingual drafting will eventually contribute to the development of the unified "Canadian style" predicted by Elmer Driedger.

These drafting conventions are expressed as rules, but the reader must bear in mind that they are intended primarily as a guide. It will often be necessary to make exceptions or to adapt the spirit of the conventions to particular circumstances.

It is perhaps inevitable that drafting conventions deal primarily with matters of form. However, as drafters of legislation we are concerned as much with the substantive adequacy and the logical organization of our texts as with their form.

i. General

Logical organization

1. The organization of an Act should be logical.

A logically organized text usually proceeds from the general to the particular and follows the chronological sequence of events. If it deals with matters that occur in a particular order, such as court proceedings of administrative applications, that order should normally be followed. See also Part III on logical arrangement.

Style

2. An Act should be written simply, clearly and concisely, with the required degree of precision, and as much as possible in ordinary language.

Simplicity and conciseness of language can be made to exist with precision in a well organized text. It is important not to exaggerate the degree of precision that is required.

Sex-specific references

3. Sex-specific references should be avoided.

In the English version of an Act, pronouns such as "he", "his" and "him" should not be used if the message is intended to refer to persons of either sex. Instead, the drafter can use "he or she", repeat the noun referred to or use a combination of these methods. Typographical devices such as brackets, virgules and hyphens are unseemly and distracting and should not be used. It is usually possible to restructure sentences so as to avoid the problem altogether.

Nouns that have the appearance of referring to men only should be replaced by terms that can refer to both sexes (for example, use "firefighter" instead of "fireman").

Because French nouns have grammatical rather than natural gender, and because in that language adjectives and past participles must agree with the nouns to which they relate, French solutions to the problems of sex-specific references are necessarily different from those used in the English version. See the French commentary on this point.

ii. Divisions of an Act

Required elements

4. (1) An Act always has a title and one or more sections (numbered 1, 2, 3 . . .).

The statutes and ordinances of all Canadian jurisdictions always contain an enacting clause an element that is not found in Uniform Acts.

Optional elements

(2) An Act may also contain the following elements:

(a) a preamble;

(b) parts (designated Part I, Part II . . .);
(c) schedules (designated Schedule I, Schedule II . . .);
(d) forms (designated Form 1, Form 2 . . .).

On the subject of preambles, see section 18.

If there is only one schedule or form, it is not necessary to number it.

Subdivisions of sections

(3) A section may be subdivided into subsections (numbered (1), (2), (3) . . .).

(4) A section that is not subdivided into subsections and a subsection may be subdivided into clauses (lettered (a), (b), (c) . . .).

(5) A clause may be subdivided into subclauses (numbered (i), (ii), (iii) . . .).

(6) A subclause may be subdivided into paragraphs (lettered (A), (B), (C) . . .).

Excessive subdivision into clauses, subclauses and paragraphs should be avoided as it makes the text harder to understand. See subsection 30(1).

Definitions

5. Definitions form part of a section or subsection and are separated by semicolons. They begin with a lower-case letter and are not lettered or numbered. Subdivisions, if any, within an individual definition take the form of clauses and are indented, separated by commas, and identified as (a), (b), and so forth.

In bilingual Acts, because definitions are arranged alphabetically in each language, a system of cross-references is necessary. It is recommended that the corresponding term in the other language be shown in brackets at the end of each definition.

There are conventional differences between French and English usage in the form of definitions.

The following example shows the recommended form of a provision containing a series of definitions:

> 1. In this Act,
> "Minister" means the Minister of Agriculture; ("Ministre")
> "weed" means dandelion, ragweed or thistle. ("mauvaise herbe")

Form of sections and their subdivisions

6. Sections and subsections begin with a capital letter and end with a period. Clauses are indented, begin with a lower-case letter and are separated by semicolons. Subclauses are further indented, begin with a lower-case letter and are separated by commas. Paragraphs are still further indented, begin with a lower case letter and are separated by commas.

The "paragraph" used by some jurisdictions requires introductory words like "the following" followed by a colon. The paragraphs are indented and numbered with Arabic numerals. They begin with an upper-case letter and are separated by a period. Like clauses, they must be grammatically parallel, but they may consist of complete sentences or of fragments. The "paragraph" is more autonomous than the clause, which must be an integral part of a single sentence.

iii. Arrangement

Preamble

7. If a preamble is to be included, it follows the title.

Definitions

8. Definitions should be set out in the first section of the Act, unless they apply only to a particular Part, section or group of sections. In that case, they should be placed at the beginning of the passage in question.

Interpretation or application provisions

9. Provisions that deal with the interpretation or application of the Act should follow the definitions.

Regulation-making powers

10. Provisions conferring regulation-making powers should come at the end of the Act, preceding only the transitional or temporary provisions, those repealing or amending other Acts and the commencement provision.

If an Act is divided into Parts, it may be more practical to group the provisions conferring regulation-making powers at the end of the individual Parts to which they relate.

Transitional or temporary provisions

11. Transitional or temporary provisions should follow the subject-matter to which they relate.

If they relate to the Act as a whole, they should follow the regulation-making powers.

Repealing and amending provisions

12. Provisions repealing or amending other Acts should precede the commencement provision.

Commencement provisions

13. The provision dealing with the coming into force of the Act should be its last section.

Schedules

14. Schedules, if they are necessary, should follow the last section of the Act.

It may be helpful to mention, in the heading of the schedule, the section to which it refers. The same is true in the case of forms (see section 15).

Forms

15. Forms, if it is necessary to include them in the Act, should be placed at the end of the Act, following the schedules, if any.

Normally, it is preferable to leave forms to be prescribed by regulation or by administrative procedures.

Marginal notes and table of contents

16. (1) Each section should have a succinct marginal note.

(2) A table of contents setting out the marginal note for each section may be inserted between the title and first section of the Act.

A table of contents is useful for the drafter as well as for the reader, since its preparation requires further review of the Act's basic structure and exposes any flaws in its logical organization.

However, it the Act is very short, a table of contents is not necessary.

iv. Drafting Principles

Title

17. The title should succinctly indicate the Act's subject-matter.

Preamble

18. The use of preambles is not recommended.

Statement of purpose

19. If a statement of purpose is required, it should be structured as a section rather than as a preamble.

Explicit statements of purpose are rarely necessary, since the object of a well-drafted Act should become clear to the person who reads it as a whole. In general, legislation should not contain statements of a non-legislative nature. However, a specific statement of purpose is occasionally required (for example, to give guidance to the courts).

Parts

20. An act should be divided into Parts only if the subject-matter of each Part is clearly distinct.

The insertion of succinct headings before groups of related sections may be useful alternative for supplement to division into Parts.

Definitions

21. (1) Definitions should be used sparingly and only for the following purposes:

(a) to establish that a term is not being used in a usual meaning, or is being used in only one of several usual meanings;
(b) to avoid excessive repetition;
(c) to allow the use of an abbreviation;
(d) to signal the use of an unusual or novel term.

The drafter should not prepare the definitions until the main substantive provisions of the Act have been settled.

See also section 32.

No substantive content

(2) A definition should not have any substantive content.

Statements of the application of the Act should be made in substantive provisions rather than definitions.

Artificiality

(3) A definition should not give an artificial or unnatural sense to the tem defined.

"Means" and "includes"

(4) "Means" and "includes" have different uses.

Note that the French version of this subsection is different.

"Means" is appropriate for exhaustive definition (where French uses s'entend de, or no linking word at all). "Includes" is appropriate for two kinds of definitions; those that extend the defined term's usual meaning (here French uses techniques such as assimiler à), and those that merely give examples of the defined term's meaning without being exhaustive (here, French generally uses s'entend notamment de). When a bilingual Act is being prepared, the two drafters must consider the issues together.

The drafter should exercise caution when using "includes". It should not be used in exhaustive definitions, and the contradictory "means and includes" should never be used.

Consistency

(5) A defined term should never be used in the same Act in a different sense.

See also subsection 34(2).

Content of section

22. (1) A section should deal with a single idea or with a group of closely related ideas.

Single Sentence

(2) A section (or, if it is divided into subsections, each subsection) should consist of a single sentence.

Short sentence

(3) Sentences should be as short as clarity and precision will allow.

Note that the French version of subsection 24(2) is different.

The tradition of one-sentence sections is not generally followed in French drafting, where a series of short sentences are often preferred to a single long one.

In both languages, it is desirable to keep sentences terse and simple. (In traditional English drafting, the one-sentence rule has often led to excessively long sentences.) If a sentence becomes long and convoluted, the drafter should first consider whether it contains redundant material and can be simplified or (if there is no redundancy) whether it would be more appropriate to break it into two or more subsections. The French drafter may also resort to the technique of creating two or more sentences within the original provision.

In a bilingual Act, although the French version of a section or subsection may contain two or more sentences and the English only one, the formal structure of both versions must remain the same (for example, it would not be acceptable to have two subsections in one version and three in the other).

Use of clauses and further subdivisions

23. (1) Clauses should be used only if they improve communication of the message to the reader. Subclauses and paragraphs should be used even more sparingly.

"Clause sandwiches"

(2) "Clause sandwiches" should be avoided.

Arrangements of a flush passage followed by a series of clauses and a closing flush are undesirable. Even more undesirable are similar arrangements containing two series of clauses, interrupted by a flush passage. They are apt to lead the drafter into errors of grammar and logic, and are difficult to read in either language. In bilingual drafting, "clause sandwiches" make it difficult sometimes impossible to ensure close correspondence of form between the two versions.

Parallelism

(3) Clauses and further subdivisions should be grammatically and logically parallel to one another.

Connection words

(4) A series of clauses or further subdivisions should usually be linked by one "and" or "or", placed at the end of the second-last item in the series.

No conjunction should be used if the subdivisions follow a complete sentence (e.g. "The court may give directions with respect to the following matters: . . . ."). It is best to omit "and" and "or" if their use could cause confusion.

Note that the French version of this subsection is different.

In French drafting, the fact that the series is conjunctive or disjunctive is indicated by appropriate introductory words, not by literal equivalents of "and" and "or".

Verbs in present indicative

24. (1) Verbs should appear in the present tense and indicative mood unless the context requires an exception.

The use of "shall" as an imperative is the major exception to this rule.

Passive undesirable

(2) Restraint should be exercised in the use of the passive voice.

Duties and prohibitions

(3) "Shall" is used to impose a duty or (with "not" or "no") a prohibition.

Powers, rights and choices

(4) "May" is used to confer or indicate a power, right or choice.

Note that the French versions of subsections (3) and (4) are different.

In French drafting, an obligation is usually imposed by the present indicative form of the verb, occasionally by auxiliaries such as doit or est tenu de. A prohibition is indicated by the use of the auxiliary *ne peut*, by *il est interdit de* or sometimes by the auxiliary *ne doit*. A power, right or choice is indicated by the auxiliary *peut* or occasionally by other phrases.

Internal references

25. Internal references should be used sparingly.

A logical arrangement makes frequent internal references unnecessary.

Internal references should clearly identify the provisions referred to by their number or letter. It is not necessary to describe the provision referred to as "of this Act", unless there is a danger of confusion with another Act that has been mentioned.

Derogations and restrictions

26. (1) Derogations and restrictions ("notwithstanding", "despite" and "subject to") should be used sparingly and only if there is an inconsistency, to make it clear which provision is meant to prevail.

Inconsistencies can often be eliminated by reading the passage.

(2) If provision 1 is meant to prevail over provision 2, it is sufficient to say that 1 applies notwithstanding (or despite) 2, or that 2 is subject to 1. The two devices should not be used simultaneously.

Placement of new provisions

27. (1) A new provision should be inserted in the most logical place.

Designation of new provisions

(2) The numbers or letters assigned to new provisions are determined in accordance with the decimal system adopted by the Conference (1968 Proceedings pages 76-89).

Changes to original structure

(3) Amendments to existing Acts should not detract from the readability of the original structure.

Rather than attaching new provisions to an existing structure, perhaps repeatedly, it may be desirable to rework the original structure.

Tables and mathematical formulas

28. Tables and mathematical formulas should be used if they make the text clearer and more concise.

Regulation-making powers

29. Regulation-making powers should be clearly expressed and should be no broader than is necessary.

v. Language

Ordinary language

30. (1) An Act should be written as much as possible in ordinary language, using technical terminology only if precision requires it.

Intended audience

(2) The terminology of an Act should be suitable for its intended audience.

Redundancies and archaisms

31. Redundant or archaic words and phrases should be avoided.

It is desirable to examine stock phrases that take the form of pairs or triplets (especially common in English for example, "give, devise and bequeath", "terms and conditions") in order to determine whether fewer words could convey the desired meaning. Legislation should be written in a style that is correct and up to date without being either faddish or excessively conservative. Many words and phrases that are often seen in legal documents belong to an earlier age and are no longer well understood. They should be replaced by a contemporary equivalent. If they add nothing to the message, as is often the case, they should be eliminated.

Neologisms

32. Neologisms should be used with caution.

In principle, terms that are not found in standard reference works should be avoided in legislation. Sometimes it is necessary to invent a term or to use a recently coined term; in which case it is prudent to define it. The use of neologisms causes special problems in bilingual drafting.

Note that in bilingual common law jurisdictions, often the use of neologisms is the only way to express in French with precision legal concepts that are derived from English law and lack any satisfactory French "functional equivalent".

Other languages

33. Terms from languages other than English should be used only if they are generally understood and if there is no equally clear and concise way of expressing the concept in English.

Latin and other foreign terms are used even less often in French than in English.

Consistency

34. (1) Different terms should not be used to express the same meaning within a single Act.

(2) The same term should not be used with different meanings within a single Act, unless, in a given context, the particular meaning that is intended is perfectly clear and no other term is suitable.

The exception does not apply to defined terms, which should never be used in a different sense than that of the definition. See subsection 21(5).

vi. Bilingual Drafting

Bilingual legislation should be prepared by two drafters, one responsible for each version, who co-operate on a basis of equality.

Ideally, both drafters should be bilingual. The participation of linguists and translators is often helpful.

Although it is usually faster and may seem easier to conduct the drafting process in only one language and to prepare a translation once the unilingual draft is settled, the quality of both versions is significantly improved by co-drafting.

Substance

35. The English and French versions of a bilingual Act must be identical in substance.

Linguistic quality

36. Each version should be written in correct and idiomatic language, and neither version should be forcibly adjusted to fit the peculiarities of the other language.

In bilingual drafting, both drafters must be ready to make necessary compromises in order to reconcile the need for linguistic quality with the need for identity of substance and close correspondence of structure.

Structure

37. (1) The structure of the Act should be the same in both versions.

Parallelism at the structural level promotes identity of substance. It is likewise a valuable tool for the increasing number of bilingual users and interpreters of the law who compare the two versions.

Acceptable differences

(2) It is not necessary that corresponding English and French provisions use the same syntax.

(3) One version of a subsection (or of a section that contains no subsections) may contain a different number of sentences than the other.

(4) Occasionally, a definition that is present in one version may not be necessary in the other.

ANNEX 2

The Uniform Law Conference of Canada Model Interpretation Act[1]

UNIFORM LAW CONFERENCE OF CANADA
CIVIL LAW SECTION

MODEL INTERPRETATION ACT
AND COMMENTARIES

Adopted December 2015

MODEL INTERPRETATION ACT

Part 1 – General

Interpretation

1(1) In this Act:

"enact" includes issue, make, establish or prescribe;

"repeal" includes revoke, cancel or rescind.

(2) An enactment that has expired, is no longer authorized or has otherwise ceased to have effect is deemed repealed for the purposes of this Act.

COMMENTARY — In this Model Act (MA) "enact" and "repeal" are only intended to apply to the Model Act (MA). Section 34 of the MA contains definitions that are applicable to all Acts and statutory instruments.

COMMENTARY — The following may be a useful provision to authorize the express repeal of enactments referred to in the proposed subsection (2). If the provision is only to apply to "regulations" then this provision should be included in the Act that deals with the filing and publishing of regulations.

Consider: — (x) The Lieutenant Governor in Council [Governor in Council] may repeal a statutory instrument that has expired, is no longer authorized or has otherwise ceased to have effect even though the statutory instrument being repealed was made by a member of the Executive Council or some other body or person.

Application

2 Every provision of this Act applies to every enactment, whenever enacted, unless a contrary intention appears in this Act or in an enactment.

COMMENTARY — In most jurisdictions in Canada and Australia, only "contrary intention" is referred to. In other jurisdictions, including Ontario, similar provisions also include "its application would give to a term or provision a meaning that is inconsistent with the context" or similar wording. It was not necessary to include "context", as contrary intention can be determined by context.

Part 2 – Coming into force and Repeal of Enactments

Date of coming into force of Acts

3(1) An Act or portion of an Act comes into force on the date or in the manner specified in the Act.

(2) If no date or manner of coming into force is specified, the Act or portion comes into force on the date the Act receives Royal Assent.

(3) If a provision of an Act states that the Act or a portion of the Act is to come into force by order of the Lieutenant Governor in Council [Governor in Council], on a specified date or in a specified manner, that provision comes into force on the date the Act receives Royal Assent.

(4) An order referred to in subsection (3),

(a) may apply to the coming into force of any provision of the Act or portion, and

(b) may be issued at different times for different provisions of the Act or portion.

COMMENTARY

1 – Instead of referring to an Act or a provision coming into force on Proclamation, only an order in council (OC) is required. BC brings their legislation into force by Regulation. A Proclamation requires 2 steps. 1 – an OC to authorize the Proclamation and 2 – the issuance of the Proclamation.

2 – Saskatchewan and Alberta have separate provisions for repealing an Act on Proclamation. There are at least 2 instances where

repealing an Act (or provision of an Act) on Proclamation may be useful:

A – Where it is known that a piece of legislation will only be in effect for a short period, but the exact date is uncertain, then the Act can be repealed without going back to the House.

B – To phase-in a new Act. This approach could be useful so that portions of an Act to be replaced can still remain in force before similar provisions in the new enactment are to come into force. However situations like this are better dealt with by "transitional" provisions.

Date of coming into force of statutory instruments

4 (1) A statutory instrument or a portion of a statutory instrument comes into force on the date or in the manner specified in the statutory instrument.

(2) If no date or manner of the coming into force is specified, the statutory instrument or portion comes into force on the date on which it is enacted.

(3) Subsections (1) and (2) apply to a regulation only if the regulation is exempt from [filing] [deposit] [registration] under [the *Regulations Act/Statutory Instruments Act, etc.*].

COMMENTARY—Depending on the scope of a revised "Model Regulations Act", section 4 could be included in that Act.

Effective time of coming into force and repeal

5 Unless otherwise provided,

(a) an enactment comes into force at the beginning of the day on which it comes into force, and

(b) the repeal of an enactment takes effect at the beginning of the day of the repeal.

COMMENTARY — The current Uniform Interpretation Act (UIA) provision provides as follows:

"5 An enactment takes effect on the first moment of the day on which it comes into force."

While it does not expressly deal with when a repeal takes effect, it was likely intended to be at the beginning of the day.

In previous versions of the UIA and currently in many jurisdictions the Act comes into force at the beginning of the day but the repeal takes effect at the end of the day.

The advantage of the proposed rule is that the rules for coming into force and repeal are the same. In those jurisdictions where the repeal is at the end of the day a third rule was necessary to deal with when an enactment is repealed and replaced. Is it the beginning of the day or is it the end of the day.

Exercise of delegated power before coming into force

6 A power in an enactment to enact a statutory instrument, or to do any other thing, may be exercised before the enactment comes into force but, except as is necessary to make the enactment effective when it comes into force, the statutory instrument enacted or other thing done has no effect until the enactment comes into force.

Effect of repeal of enactment

7(1) The repeal of an enactment does not

COMMENTARY — the current UIA (s30(a) reads as follows:

(a) revive an enactment **or thing** not in force or existing immediately before the time when the repeal takes effect,

"or thing" has been replaced with "or a law".

(a) revive an enactment that is no longer in force, or a law that no longer exists, immediately before the time the repeal takes effect,

(b) affect the previous operation of the repealed enactment,

(c) affect a right, privilege, obligation or liability that came into existence under the repealed enactment and exists immediately before the time the repeal takes effect,

(d) affect a contravention of the repealed enactment or any penalty, forfeiture or punishment incurred in connection with the contravention, or

(e) affect an investigation, proceeding or remedy in respect of

(i) a right, privilege, obligation or liability referred to in paragraph (c), or

(ii) a penalty, forfeiture or punishment referred to paragraph (d).

(2) An investigation or proceeding referred to in paragraph (1)(e) may be commenced or continued and a remedy referred to in that paragraph may be enforced as if the enactment had not been repealed.

(3) Subject to subsection 8(5), a penalty, forfeiture or punishment referred to in paragraph (1)(d) may be imposed as if the enactment had not been repealed.

COMMENTARY — Subsection (3) is not in the current UIA. It makes it clear that a penalty, forfeiture or punishment may still be imposed even if the enactment has been repealed.

Effect of repeal and substitution

8(1) In this section,

"former enactment" means an enactment that has been

(a) repealed and replaced with a new enactment, or

(b) substantially amended;

"new enactment" means an enactment that replaces a former enactment, and includes a substantial amendment to a former enactment.

(2) A person authorized to act under a former enactment may continue to act under the new enactment until another person is authorized to do so.

(3) A proceeding commenced under a former enactment must be continued under the new enactment in conformity with the procedures established by the new enactment, insofar as is practicable.

(4) Procedures established by a new enactment must be followed, with the necessary modifications, in relation to a matter that arose under the former enactment, including, without limitation,

(a) procedures for the recovery or enforcement of penalties and forfeitures incurred under the former enactment,

(b) procedures for the enforcement of a right or privilege that exists when the new enactment comes into force, or

(c) proceedings relating to matters that arose under the former enactment that are commenced after the repeal of the former enactment.

(5) If a penalty, forfeiture or punishment authorized under a former enactment is reduced or mitigated by the new enactment, the new enactment applies to any sanction imposed after the new enactment comes into force in respect of a matter that occurred under the former enactment.

(6) A statutory instrument enacted under a former enactment remains in force and is deemed to have been enacted under the new enactment insofar as it is authorized by and not inconsistent with the new enactment.

(7) If

(a) a former enactment conferred a power on a person or body to enact a statutory instrument, and

(b) the power or substantially the same power is conferred by the new enactment on a different person or body,

the person or body referred to in paragraph (b) has the power to repeal, amend or replace the statutory instrument enacted by the person or body referred to in paragraph (a).

Included powers — statutory instruments

9 A power to enact a statutory instrument includes the power, exercisable in the same manner and subject to the same conditions, if any, to repeal or amend the statutory instrument.

Part 3 — Interpretation of Enactments

Enactment remedial

10 (1) The words of an Act and regulations authorized under an Act are to be read in their entire context, and in their grammatical and ordinary sense, harmoniously with the scheme of the Act, the object of the Act and the intention of Parliament.

(2) Acts and regulations are to be construed as being remedial and are to be given the fair, large and liberal interpretation that best ensures the attainment of their objects.

COMMENTARY — It was decided that both subsections (1) and (2) be included. Currently only subsection (2) appears in the current UIA. Concerns were also raised that the modern principle would evolve and be reworded, or replaced by some other principle.

Enactments apply in the present

11 An enactment is to be construed as applying to circumstances as they arise.

Rolling incorporation of domestic enactments

12 (1) In this section, "domestic enactment" means an enactment of the Province, Canada, a Territory or another province of Canada.

(2) A reference in an enactment to a domestic enactment is a reference to the domestic enactment as amended or to the domestic enactment that replaced it.

(3) Subsection (2) applies whether the domestic enactment is amended or replaced before or after the coming into force of the enactment in which the reference to the domestic enactment appears.

(4) A reference in an enactment to a domestic enactment that has been repealed and not replaced is a reference to the domestic enactment as it read immediately before its repeal.

Static incorporation of foreign enactment

13 (1) In this section, "foreign enactment" means an enactment of a jurisdiction outside Canada.

(2) A reference in an enactment to a foreign enactment is a reference to the foreign enactment as it read on the date on which the enactment containing the reference was enacted.

COMMENTARY — Section 62 of the Ontario Act deals with the incorporation by reference of non-legislative documents. The provision is not an interpretive provision. It authorizes under certain conditions the ability of regulations to incorporate these types of documents.

Amending enactments

14 An amending enactment is to be construed as part of the enactment that it amends.

No implication from repeal, amendment, etc.

15 (1) The repeal of an enactment, the repeal and replacement of an enactment or the amendment of an enactment is not to be construed to be or to involve

(a) a declaration that the enactment was or was considered by the Legislature or other body or person by whom it was enacted to have been previously in force, or

(b) a declaration as to the previous state of the law.

(2) The amendment of an enactment is not to be construed to be or to involve a declaration that the law under the enactment prior to the amendment was or was considered by the Legislature or other body or person who enacted it to be different from the law under the enactment as amended.

(3) A re-enactment in the same words, revision, consolidation or amendment of an enactment is not to be construed to be or to involve an adoption of the construction that has by judicial decision or otherwise been placed on the language used in the enactment or on similar language.

References to statutory instruments

16 A reference in an enactment to a statutory instrument is a reference to a statutory instrument made under the enactment.

Common names

17 If the name commonly applied to a country, place, body, corporation, society, officer, functionary, person, party or thing is used in an enactment, that name means the country, place, body, corporation, society, officer, functionary, person, party or thing to which the name is commonly applied, even though that name is not the formal or extended designation of it.

Bilingual texts

18 The English and French versions of an enactment that is enacted in both languages are equally authoritative.

COMMENTARY — If the jurisdiction has an Act that deals with "languages", this section likely belongs there. Note that the NWT *Official Languages Act* allows for the possibility of First Nation's language translations of statutes and instruments. Nunavut's *Official Languages Act* makes an Inuktitut dialect translation a prerequisite to the introduction of bills and allows for the possibility of authoritative Inuit language versions of statutes and instruments.

Preambles and reference aids

19 (1) In this section, "section heading" means a heading that appears in an enactment immediately above or beside a section or a provision of a section.

(2) The following are part of an enactment:
(a) a preamble;
(b) headings other than section headings.

(3) The following are not part of an enactment and are to be considered to have been included editorially and for convenience of reference only:
(a) section headings;
(b) tables of contents;
(c) information notes providing legislative history;
(d) information notes providing text as an alternative for non-text content.

COMMENTARY — Paragraph (3)(c) is only recommended if historical notes are in the bill when enacted or are in the official version.

Paragraph (3)(d) may be necessary where text is provided to identify and describe non-text content (such as diagrams and maps) to assist people who use screen readers. Such alternative text is required under the Web Content Accessibility Guidelines (WCAG) to improve accessibility for people with disabilities.

Each jurisdiction may have different terminology for types of headings.

The courts are already looking at reference aids. The intention here is not to try to tell the Courts what they can consider in interpreting the Act but simply to state what does and does not constitute part of the Act. Arguably, if it's not part of the Act, it can be amended editorially; but the provision does not preclude the courts from looking at them. It's for this reason that "section headings (marginal notes)" fall into the category of not being part of the Act.

Government bound by enactments — exception

20 (1) An enactment is binding on the Crown.

(2) Exceptions . . .

COMMENTARY — Under the current UIA and in most of the jurisdictions (except PEI and BC), the Crown is not bound unless the enactment states that the Crown is bound. Under section 20 the presumption is reversed.

BC has included an exception as follows:

> *Despite subsection (1), an enactment that would bind or affect the government in the use or development of land, or in the planning, construction, alteration, servicing, maintenance or use of improvements, as defined in the Assessment Act does not bind or affect the government.*

In PEI there weren't any exceptions however the provision only applied to new legislation.

In 1989 the Ontario law Reform Commission of Ontario recommended a reversal of the presumption. More recently both the Alberta Law Reform Institute and the Law Reform Commission of Saskatchewan have also recommended the reversal of the presumption, with possible exceptions. For example: the Crown as creditor; planning legislation; Crown as witness.

Succession

21 A change of reigning sovereign does not affect anything done or begun under the previous reigning sovereign and all matters continue as if no succession had occurred.

COMMENTARY — Some jurisdictions may have this provision in another Act — Demise of the Crown Act, Judicature Act, etc.

Appointments

22 (1) Authority under an enactment to appoint a person to an office includes the authority to

(a) appoint the person either for a fixed term or during pleasure,
(b) provide for the appointee's remuneration,
(c) provide for payment of the appointee's expenses,
(d) remove or suspend the appointee,
(e) reappoint or reinstate the person as appointee,
(f) appoint a deputy who has the same powers as the appointee
  (i) subject to the conditions, or

(ii) with the limitation of powers as may be specified in the appointment, and

(g) temporarily appoint another person to act in the office if

(i) the office is vacant,

(ii) the appointee is absent or unable to act for any reason, including, without limitation, illness or incapacity or a conflict of interest in respect of a matter, or

(iii) the appointee gives prior notice of a temporary absence or resignation, such appointment to take effect on the office becoming vacant.

(2) An appointment during pleasure may be revoked at any time without cause or notice.

(3) An appointment is effective at the beginning of the day on which the appointment is to take effect.

(4) Subject to subsection (5), an appointment for a term that is to conclude, expire or otherwise come to an end on a specified day includes that day.

(5) An appointment that is terminated, revoked or rescinded effective on a specified day is effective at the beginning of the specified day.

COMMENTARY — Not all jurisdictions have specific provisions like section 22(3) to (5), which deal with when appointments expire and when they take effect. Some jurisdictions rely on the computation of time provisions or the date of coming into force of enactments provisions.

In BC, for example, all appointments commence at the beginning of the day and also expire/terminate at the beginning of the day.

The current UIA, and most jurisdictions that currently have similar provisions, provide that the appointment expires at the end of the day. In addition though, a further provision is needed to deal with what happens when an appointment is terminated before it expires. In Alberta, for example, if an appointment is terminated before it expires, it expires at the beginning of the day [see proposed 22(5)].

Corporations — included powers

23 (1) An enactment establishing or continuing a corporation is to be construed as vesting in the corporation the authority to

(a) have perpetual succession,
(b) sue and be sued in its corporate name,
(c) contract and be contracted with in its corporate name,
(d) have a common seal and alter or change it, and
(e) acquire, hold and dispose of personal property for its purposes.

(2) An enactment establishing or continuing a corporation is to be construed as

(a) vesting in the majority of its members the ability to bind the others, and
(b) exempting its individual members from personal liability for the corporation's debts, obligations or acts who do not contravene the enactment.

(3) This section applies to an enactment only if the enactment is in force on the date this section comes into force.

COMMENTARY — Section 16 of the UIA was not retained. While it is written as an interpretive provision, it is substantive in nature. Statutory corporations that are now being established are more complex than they used to be. This provision has been carried forward since at least 1859. Jurisdictions shouldn't continue relying on this provision. It is recommended that the Ontario Act (section 92) be followed where their equivalent section 16 only applies to corporations established before the new Interpretation Act came into force. BC and NS Interpretation Acts seem to cover all corporations while others only apply to corporations established by an enactment.

Included powers — generally

24 (1) If an enactment confers a power, all the powers that are necessary to exercise the power are also conferred.

(2) If in an enactment the performance of an authorized action is dependent on the Lieutenant Governor in Council or a person

performing another action, the Lieutenant Governor in Council or the person has the power to perform that other action.

Gender specific references

25 In an enactment, gender-specific words refer to any gender and include corporations.

Number specific references

26 In an enactment, words in the singular include the plural and words in the plural include the singular.

Delegation

27 (1) If an enactment authorizes the holder of an office or position to delegate a power granted or a duty imposed on the office or position by the enactment, the holder, despite any delegation made, may exercise the power or perform the duty.

(2) A delegation made under the authority of an enactment remains valid and in effect until the delegation is revoked or expires unless

(a) the enactment providing the delegated power or duty is repealed or so changed in substance that the power or duty is not substantially the same, or

(b) the enactment authorizing the delegation is repealed or so changed in substance that the delegation is no longer authorized.

(3) An authority conferred by an Act to delegate a power or duty does not include the power to delegate a power to make regulations unless specifically authorized.

Acting minister or other statutory officer

28 (1) Words in an enactment directing or empowering a minister include

(a) a minister acting for the minister,

(b) the minister's deputy or associate deputy, and

(c) a person employed in the minister's department in an appropriate capacity.

(2) Words in an enactment directing or empowering the holder of a position or an office, other than a judicial office, referred to in the enactment include

(a) a person appointed to act for the holder,
(b) the holder's deputy, and
(c) a person employed in the holder's organization in an appropriate capacity.

(3) For certainty, if a power or duty referred to in subsection (1) or (2) is delegated under a statutory power of delegation, those subsections do not apply in respect of the power or duty.

(4) Subsections (1) and (2) apply whether or not the office or position is vacant.

(5) Subsections (1) and (2) apply whether the power or duty is administrative, judicial or legislative or involves the holding of an opinion or the reaching of a conclusion.

(6) Despite this section, a power to make regulations conferred by an Act may be exercised only by the minister or other person upon whom the power is conferred by the Act.

COMMENTARY — The Model Act follows the Saskatchewan provision, which further clarifies and expands the Carltona Doctrine and the implied devolution of power. The Federal Interpretation Act, which has a similar provision, does not extend beyond the ministerial level.

While delegation provisions provide significantly more certainty, Carltona could be relied on in the absence of a delegation in writing. Under this common law exception, the statutory power is not exercised by the subordinate in his or her own right. Rather, the subordinate is deemed to exercise the power for and on behalf of the person or body in whom the power was originally vested. The original power holder remains responsible and accountable.

Power to differentiate

29 A power to make a statutory instrument includes the power to make statutory instruments that

(a) are general or particular in application,
(b) are different for different classes, and
(c) establish classes for the purposes of paragraph (b).

COMMENTARY — Jurisdictions may want to restrict the operation of the provision to regulations, rather than statutory instruments.

Deviations from required form

30 If an enactment requires the use of a specified form, deviations from the form do not invalidate a form used if

(a) the deviations do not affect the substance,
(b) the deviations are not likely to mislead, and
(c) the form used is organized in the same way or substantially the same way as the form the use of which is required.

COMMENTARY — This provision will have to ensure that it works with forms that are required to be submitted in electronic form.

Defined terms

31 If a word or expression is defined in an enactment, other parts of speech and grammatical forms of the same word or expression have corresponding meanings.

COMMENTARY — Section 14 of the UIA has been omitted as no longer being necessary.

14 Definitions or interpretation provisions in an enactment shall be construed as being applicable to the whole enactment including the section containing the definitions or interpretation provision

Terms used in statutory instruments

32 A word or expression used in a statutory instrument has the same meaning as in the enactment authorizing the statutory

instrument, whether or not the word or expression is defined in the authorizing enactment.

Computation of time

33 (1) A period of time expressed in days and described as beginning or ending on, at or with a specified day includes the specified day.

(2) A period of time expressed in days and described as beginning before, after or from a specified day excludes the specified day.

(3) A period of time described by reference to a number of days between two events excludes the day on which the first event happens and includes the day on which the second event happens

(4) Subsections (1), (2) and (3) apply even if the period is expressed as "at least" or "not less than" a number of days or as requiring clear days.

(5) A time limit for the doing of anything that falls or expires on a holiday is extended to include the next day that is not a holiday.

(6) A time limit, for registering or filing documents or for doing anything else, that falls or expires on a day on which the place for doing so is not open during its regular hours of business is extended to include the next day the place is open during its regular hours of business.

(7) A period of time expressed as one or more consecutive months beginning or ending on, at, with, before, after or from a specified day, is counted to the date numerically corresponding to the date of the specified day in the last or first month of the period, as the case requires.

(8) A period of time expressed as one or more consecutive years beginning or ending on, at, with, before, after or from a specified day, is counted to the same date as the specified day in the last or first year of the period, as the case requires.

(9) If a period of time would end on a date in a month that has no date numerically corresponding to the first date in the period, the period ends on the first day of the next month.

(10) A person reaches a particular age expressed in years at the beginning of the relevant anniversary of his or her birth date.

COMMENTARIES — The distinction between "clear days" and "at least" has been eliminated. In current legislation the term "clear days" is rarely used and the distinction in using or not using "at least" is likely lost on most readers.

Definitions

34 In an enactment:

"Act" means an Act of the Legislature [Parliament] and includes an ordinance of . . .–
each jurisdiction would include different things here;

COMMENTARY — In some jurisdictions the term "statute" is used but isn't defined and as a result could be interpreted in certain contexts as including an Act of another jurisdiction. In fact in Yukon, "statute" is defined to mean an Act of Canada or a province, including an Ordinance of the NWT and Nunavut. Each jurisdiction will need to decide if "statute" needs to be defined.

Those Provinces that were carved out of the Territories currently refer to ordinances in their definition of "Act", in the event that some ordinances still apply. Yukon, defines an Act as being an Ordinance of Yukon.

"bank" means "bank" as defined in the *Bank Act* (Canada);

"enactment" means an Act or a statutory instrument or a portion of an Act or a statutory instrument;

COMMENTARY — The reference to "regulation" has been changed to "statutory instrument". Currently the definition of "regulation" is drafted very broadly and in fact the term "regulation" is actually one of the listed instruments in the definition. In order to remedy that drafting problem, it was felt that a more "neutral" term should be used. Each jurisdiction can determine how broad they want the definition to be.

If a jurisdiction decides to use a more neutral term, this could lead to extensive amendments to their body of Acts and regulations.

"Governor", "Governor of Canada" or "Governor General" means the Governor General of Canada and includes the Administrator of Canada;

"Governor in Council" or "Governor General in Council" means the Governor-General acting on the advice and with the consent of the Queen's Privy Council for Canada;

"Her Majesty", "His Majesty", "the Queen", "the King", "the Crown" or "the Sovereign" means the Sovereign of the United Kingdom, Canada and Her other realms and territories, and Head of the Commonwealth;

"holiday" means . . .

COMMENTARY — Each jurisdiction should fill in the days appropriate to its own jurisdiction.

"Legislative Assembly" means the Legislative Assembly of [Province];

"Lieutenant Governor" means the Lieutenant Governor for [Province] and includes the Administrator of [Province];

"Lieutenant Governor in Council" means the Lieutenant Governor acting on the advice and with the consent of the Executive Council;

"person" includes a corporation;

"proclamation" means a proclamation of the Lieutenant Governor issued under the Great Seal by order of the Lieutenant Governor in Council [a proclamation under the Great Seal (Can.)];

"Province" means the Province of [ ];

"province", when used to refer to a part of Canada, includes the Territories;

COMMENTARY — May not need to include the definition if jurisdiction usually refers to both provinces and territories in its enactments.

"regulation" means a statutory instrument to which the *Regulations Act* [other Act that defines this category of regulation] applies;

"statutory declaration" or "solemn declaration" means a sworn declaration referred to in section X [69] of the *Evidence Act* (B.C.) or section 14 [or 15?] of the *Evidence Act* (Canada);

COMMENTARY — This definition may not be needed in the Interpretation Act, as it may be better placed in the Evidence Act.

"statutory instrument" means a regulation, order, rule, form, tariff of costs or fees, proclamation, letters patent, commission, bylaw, or other instrument enacted

(a) in execution of a power conferred under an Act, or

(b) by or under the authority of the Lieutenant Governor in Council,

but, for certainty, does not include an order of a court or an order made with respect to the resolution of a dispute between 2 or more persons;

"swear" includes solemnly affirm or declare;

COMMENTARY — As drafted, "statutory instrument" would be used to include all types of "statutory instruments", including law-making regulations. (See definition above "Regulation".)

"Territories" means the Northwest Territories, Nunavut and Yukon.

COMMENTARY — The definitions may need to be treated differently for legislation in the Territories. For example, " Commissioner" instead of Lieutenant Governor or Governor General; "Council" instead of "Legislative Assembly"; "Ordinance" instead of "Act or statute"

COMMENTARY — The following from the UIA have not be retained in the definition section:

"commencement"
"Great Seal"
"herein" and "hereafter" "may" and "shall" "now" and "next" "oath"
"prescribed"
"public officer"

COMMENTARY — Transitional Provisions
Jurisdictions that adopt the Model Act or portions of it will need to consider whether any transitional provisions will be necessary. Some of the proposed provisions may be a complete reversal of the jurisdictions current Act.

Notes

Introduction

1 30 & 31 Vict, c 3 (UK), ss 91–95.

2 Parliament has exercised its authority under the *Constitution Act, 1871*, 34–35 Vict, c 28 (UK) to create the territorial legislatures by Acts of Parliament: *Northwest Territories Act*, SC 2014, c 2, s 18, *Nunavut Act*, SC 1993, c 28, s 23, and *Yukon Act*, SC 2002, c 7, s 18.

3 See *Commissioner of the Northwest Territories v Canada*, 2001 FCA 220 at paras 20–22.

4 A rare example of primary legislation made under the Crown prerogative is the *Canadian Passport Order*, SI/81-86.

5 See the Legislative Drafting Conventions of the Uniform Law Conference of Canada, online: https://ulcc-chlc.ca/Civil-Section/Drafting/Drafting-Conventions.

6 Historically, sections of Acts in England began with the words "*provisum est*" (it is provided): see EA Driedger, *The Composition of Legislation*, 2d ed (Department of Justice: Ottawa, 1976) at 93.

7 RSC 1985, c C-46, Part IX.

CHAPTER ONE | What Is Drafting?

1 See below, Chapter Three: How Is Draft Legislation Turned Into Law?

2 See below, in Chapter Two: How Is Legislation Drafted? — Drafters and Drafting Offices.

3 See below, in Chapter Two: How Is Legislation Drafted? — Who Else Is Involved in Drafting?

4 See, for example, Bill C-262 in the 1st Session of the 42nd Parliament, which led to the introduction and enactment of Bill C-15 in the 2nd Session of the 43rd Parliament, enacted as SC 2021, c 14 (*United Nations Declaration of Indigenous Peoples Act*).

5 See *Guide to Making Federal Acts and Regulations*, 2d ed (Privy Council Office: Ottawa, 2001). See online: www.canada.ca/en/privy-council/services/publications/guide-making-federal-acts-regulations.html.

6 See Ministry of Justice, *A Guide to Legislation and Legislative Process in British Columbia*, online: www.crownpub.bc.ca/Product/Details/7665005851_S (Victoria: 2013).

7 See online: https://ulcc-chlc.ca/Civil-Section/Drafting/Drafting-Conventions.

8 These requirements are in the *Constitution Act, 1867*, 30 & 31 Vict, c 3, s 133, the *Manitoba Act, 1870*, s 23, the *Canadian Charter of Rights and Freedoms*, Part I of the *Constitution Act, 1982*, being Schedule B to the *Canada Act 1982* (UK), 1982, c 11, ss 17 & 18, and the *French Language Services Act*, RSO 1990, c F.32, ss 3–4.

9 See, for example, the Inuvialuit Registry of the Inuvialuit Regional Corporation in Labrador.

10 See the *Official Languages Act*, SNu 2008, c 10, s 5.

11 *Reference re Manitoba Language Rights*, [1985] 1 SCR 721 and *Attorney General of Quebec v Blaikie*, [1979] 2 SCR 1016.

12 RSC 1985, c 31 (4th Supp).

13 RSNB 1973, c O-1.

14 See for example, *French-language Services Act/Loi sur les services en français*, SNS 2004, c 26.

15 Section 110 of the *North-West Territories Act*, SC 1886, c 50, as continued by s 16 of the *Saskatchewan Act*, SC 1950, c 42, s 16, required its laws to be published in both languages, but this requirement was not constitutionally entrenched: see *R v Mercure*, [1981] 1 SCR 234; it has since been repealed. The Supreme Court has rejected arguments that the laws of Alberta were required to be published in both English and French: see *Caron v Alberta*, 2015 SCC 56.

16 RSO 1990, c F.32.

17 SO 2021, c 40, Sched 13, s 5 (amending s 4 of the *French Language Services Act*, but not yet proclaimed in force).

18 *Official Languages Act*, RSNWT 1988, c O-1, s 7; *Official Languages Act*, SNu 2008, c 10, s 5; *Languages Act*, RSY 2002, c 133, s 4. These Acts can be amended only with the concurrence of Parliament: see *Northwest Territories Act*, SC 2014, c 2, s 32; *Nunavut Act*, SC 1993, c 28, s 38; *Yukon Act*, SC 2002, c 7, s 27.

19 *Official Languages Act*, RSNWT 1988, c O-1, s 4.
20 *Official Languages Act*, SnU 2008, c 10.
21 See *ibid*, s 5.
22 See *Attorney General of Quebec v Blaikie*, [1979] 2 SCR 1016.
23 See *Reference re Manitoba Language Rights*, [1985] 1 SCR 721.
24 SS 1988-89, c L-6.1. See also *Legislation Act*, 2006, SO 2006, s 21, Sched F, s 65.
25 See also *Legislation Act*, *ibid*, s 65; *Languages Act*, RSY 2002, c 133, s 4.
26 Much has been written about this in relation to "plain language" drafting. See R Sullivan, "The Promise of Plain Language Drafting" (2001) 47 *McGill Law Journal* 97.
27 Government of Canada: Ottawa, 2001, "Chapter 1.1 — Choosing the Right Tools to Accomplish Policy Objectives," online: www.canada.ca/en/privy-council/services/publications/guide-making-federal-acts-regulations.html#pt1.
28 *R v Elm Tree Nursing Home*, (1987), 20 OAC 277 (CA).
29 See, for example, the *Income Tax Act*, RSC 1985, c 1 (5th Supp).
30 See, for example, the *Canadian Human Rights Act*, RSC 1985, c H-6.
31 30 & 31 Vict, c 3 (UK), ss 91–95.
32 *Constitution Act, 1982*, Schedule B to the *Canada Act 1982* (UK), 1982, c 11, s 52. The Constitution consists of many different pieces of legislation (listed in the Schedule to the *Constitution Act, 1982*) as well as constitutional principles, conventions, and common law.
33 See Chapter Eight: Context — Broader Legislative Context, Reconciling Conflicting Provisions.
34 SC 2020, c 5.
35 See, for example, *Interpretation Act*, RSC c I-21, s 4 and *Legislation Act, 2006*, SO 2006, c 21, Sched F, s 6.
36 See online: https://laws-lois.justice.gc.ca/PDF/2016_3.pdf.
37 SC 2001, c 27, s 1.
38 SO 2021, c 26.
39 SC 2008, c 16.
40 SC 1991, c 46.
41 *Broadcasting Act*, SC 1991, c 11, s 2.
42 *Canada–United States–Mexico Agreement Implementation Act*, SC 2020, c 1.
43 RSC 1985, c A-1. See *Canada (Office of the Information Commissioner) v Canada (Prime Minister)*, 2019 FCA 95 at para 35.
44 RSC 1985 c. I-21. See also *Legislation Act, 2006*, SO 2006, c 21, Sched F, s 51.
45 *Ibid*.
46 RSC 1985, c I-21, s 44 and *Legislation Act, 2006*, SO 2006, c 21, Sched F, s 52.
47 See, for example, *Agricultural Growth Act*, SC 2015, c 2, s 153.
48 SC 2019, c 25.

49 See, for example, *Green Energy Repeal Act, 2018*, SO 2018, c 16, s 8(10) adding s 70.9 to the *Planning Act*, RSO 1990, c P.13.
50 SC 2013, c 33.
51 SC 2000, c 32.
52 RSO 1985, c S-16.
53 SC 1997, c 26, ss. 39(2).
54 SOR/2018-83.
55 However, the Supreme Court of Canada has rejected this characterization in relation to federal legislation incorporating by reference provincial legislation: see *Coughlan v Ontario (Highway Transport Board)*, [1968] SCR 569.
56 See, for example, *Legislation Act, 2006*, SO 2006, c 21, Sched F, ss 62(3) and *Statutory Instruments Act*, RSC 1985, c S-22, ss 18.1(2).
57 See, for example, *Canadian Environmental Protection Act, 1999*, SC 1999, c 33.
58 See A Dodek, "Omnibus Bills: Constitutional Constraints and Legislative Liberations" (2017) 48 *Ottawa Law Review* 1.
59 See, for example, *Budget Implementation Act, 2021, No 1*, SC 2021, c 23, which is 368 pages and amends dozens of different Acts and regulations.
60 Renton Committee, *The Preparation of Legislation* (London: Her Majesty's Stationery Office, 1975) at 5.
61 See *Rules of Civil Procedure*, RRO 1990, Reg 194.

CHAPTER TWO | **How Is Legislation Drafted?**

1 See *House of Commons Procedure and Practice*, 3d ed (House of Commons: Ottawa, 2017), c 16 (The Legislative Process).
2 See Department of Justice, International Cooperation Group, *National Survey of Legislative Drafting Services 2002*, online: https://publications.gc.ca/collections/Collection/J2-245-2002E.pdf.
3 Ontario.
4 Nova Scotia.
5 Ontario.
6 See *Guide to Making Federal Acts and Regulations*, 2d ed (Privy Council Office: Ottawa, 2001). See online: www.canada.ca/en/privy-council/services/publications/guide-making-federal-acts-regulations.html.
7 *Ibid.*
8 See *Statutory Instruments Act*, RSC 1985, c S-22, s 3.
9 For example, in Ontario.
10 See *Guide to Making Federal Acts and Regulations*, "c 1.1 — Choosing the Right Tools to Accomplish Policy Objectives," 2d ed (Privy Council Office: Ottawa,

2001), online: www.canada.ca/en/privy-council/services/publications/guide-making-federal-acts-regulations.html.

11 SC 1960, c 44.

12 *Canadian Charter of Rights and Freedoms,* Part I of the *Constitution Act, 1982*, being Schedule B to the *Canada Act 1982* (UK), 1982, c 11.

13 For further details on co-drafting, see below, Drafting Bilingual and Bijural Legislation.

14 See Justice Laws Website, "New Layout for Legislation," online: https://laws-lois.justice.gc.ca/eng/PDF; *Canada Gazette* Part III.

15 See below, Drafting Bilingual and Bijural Legislation.

16 *Statutory Instruments Act*, RSC 1985, c S-22, s 3 and *Department of Justice Act*, RSC 1985, c J-2, s 4.1.

17 Pursuant to Standing Order 91.1 of the House of Commons, the Subcommittee on Private Members' Business of the Standing Committee on Procedure and House Affairs reviews bills placed on the Order of Precedence. Members of the House of Commons are chosen by lottery to have the opportunity to place a bill on the Order of Precedence, which ensures it will be considered at second reading. Bills on the Order of Precedence are reviewed by the Subcommittee on Private Members' Business to determine whether they are "votable" according to established criteria. Only votable bills can proceed past second reading: see *House of Commons Procedure and Practice*, 3d ed (House of Commons, 2017), c 21: online: www.ourcommons.ca/about/procedureandpractice3rdedition/ch_21_1-e.html.

18 There are many definitions of regulation. Each jurisdiction in Canada has a statute that defines regulation for publication and other procedural purposes. See, for example, the federal *Statutory Instruments Act*, RSC 1985, c S-22, s 2, Quebec's *Regulations Act*, CQLR c R-18.1, s 1, and Ontario's *Legislation Act, 2006*, SO 2006, c 21, Sched F, s 65, s 17.

19 For example, Nova Scotia, Ontario, New Brunswick, and British Columbia.

20 For example, Quebec.

21 See above, Chapter One: What Is Drafting? — Language.

22 See *Guide to Making Federal Acts and Regulations*, 2d ed, c 2.3 (Privy Council Office: Ottawa, 2001), online: www.canada.ca/en/privy-council/services/publications/guide-making-federal-acts-regulations.html.

23 See D Revell, "Authoring Bilingual Laws: The Importance of Progress" (2004) 29 *Brooklyn Journal of International Law* at 1085.

24 RSC 1985, c I-23.

25 RSC 1985, c C-44.

26 See, for example, the *Bankruptcy and Insolvency Act*, RSC 1985, c B-3, s 2.

CHAPTER THREE | How Is Draft Legislation Turned Into Law?

1 See *Constitution Act, 1867*, 30 & 31 Vict, c 3, ss 53 & 54.

2 Rules of the Senate, online: https://sencanada.ca/en/about/procedural-references/rules and Standing Orders of the House of Commons, online: www.ourcommons.ca/About/StandingOrders/Index-e.htm.

3 See, for example, the Standing Orders of the Legislative Assembly of Ontario, online: www.ola.org/en/legislative-business/standing-orders and the Nova Scotia Rules and Forms of Procedure of the House of Assembly, online: https://nslegislature.ca/sites/default/files/legc/Rules.pdf.

4 See LegisInfo.

5 Some bills are referred to committee before second reading, but this is very rare. For more detail on the multi-party composition and function of committees in the House of Commons, see *House of Commons Procedure and Practice*, 3d ed (House of Commons: Ottawa, 2017), c 20.

6 Not every bill reaches that stage. Many bills, particularly those that are not government initiatives, languish at the first reading stage until the end of a Parliament, because no motion is made to move them to second reading.

7 See *House of Commons Procedure and Practice*, above note 5, c 20.

8 *Ibid.*

9 1st Session, 42nd Parliament. Enacted as SC 2016, c 3.

10 The approximate breakdown of amendments tabled during consideration of Bill C-14 by the Standing Committee on Justice and Human Rights by members of the political parties was CPC-40; NDP-8; GP-13; LIB-10; BQ-9.

11 For more detail on Bill C-14, see online: www.parl.ca/LegisInfo/en/bill/42-1/c-14.

12 Senate Procedural Notes Number 6 Royal Assent, online: https://sencanada.ca/en/about/procedural-references/notes/n6.

13 *House of Commons Procedure and Practice*, above note 5, c 16.

14 See LegisInfo, online: www.parl.ca/legisinfo.

15 See online: https://canadagazette.gc.ca/accueil-home-eng.html; "the official newspaper of the Government of Canada [where you] can learn about new statutes, new and proposed regulations."

16 See online: https://laws-lois.justice.gc.ca/.

17 See, for example, the Ontario e-Laws site, online: www.ontario.ca/laws and the sites of other jurisdictions.

18 See the policies cited below in notes 20–21.

19 See Manitoba's Regulatory Consultation Portal for "important" regulations put forward for public comment; online: https://reg.gov.mb.ca/detail/4739117. In Alberta, proposed regulatory changes relating to the energy sector are available for public consultation, but these are tertiary instruments such

as orders, directives, and manuals. See *The Regulatory Change Report* published by the Alberta Energy Regulator, online: www.aer.ca/regulating-development/rules-and-directives/regulatory-change-report. Both Yukon and the Northwest Territories also pre-publish certain proposed regulations: see online: https://yukon.ca/en/search?query=regulatory%20policy and www.gov.nt.ca/en/engagements/proposed-regulations-corrections-act.

20 Ontario Regulatory Policy, July 2014. See online: www.ontariocanada.com/registry/downloads/Ontario%20Regulatory%20Policy.pdf.

21 BC Regulatory Reform Policy, October 2019, see online: www2.gov.bc.ca/assets/gov/government/about-the-bc-government/regulatory-reform/pdfs/regulatory_reform_policy.pdf.

22 See Quebec's *Regulations Act*, CQLR c R-18.1.

23 Treasury Board Secretariat (Ottawa, 2018). See online: www.canada.ca/en/government/system/laws/developing-improving-federal-regulations/requirements-developing-managing-reviewing-regulations/guidelines-tools/cabinet-directive-regulation.html.

24 RSC 1985, c S-22, s 3(2).

25 *Ibid*, s 3(3).

26 Part I of the *Constitution Act, 1982*, being Schedule B to the *Canada Act 1982* (UK), 1982, c 11.

27 See, for example, British Columbia's *Gazette* Part 2, BC Reg 103/2020 Order in Council 235/2020 approved and ordered 11 May 2020, amending the *Administrative Penalties Regulation*.

28 See, for example the Nunavut *Human Rights Regulations* R-001-2005 and Yukon *Bare Land Condominium Regulations*, OIC 2022/23.

29 See, for example, the *Statutory Instruments Act*, RSC 1985, c S-22, ss 5–7 and the *Legislation Act, 2006*, SO 2006, c 21, Sched F, ss 18–21.

30 See *Statutory Instruments Regulations*, CRC, c 1509, s 7.

31 See, for example, the *Statutory Instruments Act*, RSC 1985, c S-22, s 10 and the *Legislation Act, 2006*, SO 2006, c 21, Sched F, s 25.

32 See online: www.canlii.org/en.

33 Ontario, Quebec, and Saskatchewan have a regulatory review process, as does the federal jurisdiction.

34 See, for example, *First Report of the Standing Joint Committee on the Scrutiny of Regulations*, 43rd Parliament, 2nd Sess, 22 March 2021.

35 SO 2006, c 21, Sched F. See also Standing Order 111(i) of the Standing Orders of the Legislative Assembly of Ontario.

36 *Legislation Act, 2006*, SO 2006, c 21, Sched F, s 33(3).

37 See, for example, the Committee's *First Report 2019* and *First Report 2020* of the 1st Sess, 42nd Parliament indicating it reviewed a total of 537 regulations

made in 2018, wrote to ministries for ten of them, and reported three to the Legislative Assembly.

38 See *Regulations Act*, CQLR, c R-18.1, s 21, *Statutes and Regulations Act*, CCSM c S207, s 22(30), and *The Legislation Act*, SS 2019, c L-10.2, ss 4–16.

39 See, for example, Rule 3 of the *Federal Courts Rules*, SOR/98-106, which says:

> 3 These Rules shall be interpreted and applied
> (a) so as to secure the just, most expeditious and least expensive determination of every proceeding;

40 See IH Jacob, "The Inherent Jurisdiction of the Court" (1970) *Current Legal Problems* 23 and J Pinsler, "The Inherent Powers of the Court" [1997] *Singapore Journal of Legal Studies* 1 at 14.

41 See, for example, *Criminal Code*, RSC 1985, c C-46, s 482.

42 See, for example, the *Federal Courts Act*, RSC 1985, c F-7, s 45.1 and the *Courts of Justice Act*, RSO 1990, c C.43, s 65.

43 See, for example, *Canada Labour Code*, RSC 1985, c L-2, s 15(a).

44 See, for example, *Courts of Justice Act*, RSO 1990, c C.43, s 66 and *Competition Tribunal Act*, RSC 1985, c 19 (2nd Supp), s 16.

45 See, for example, the definition of "regulation" in the *Statutory Instruments Act*, RSC 1985, c S-23, s 2.

46 For example, Justice Laws Website and e-Laws.

47 See, for example, *Municipal Act, 2001*, SO 2001, c 25, ss 9–11 and the *Local Governance Act*, SNB 2017, c 18, ss 10–20.

48 See, for example, *City of Ottawa Act, 1999*, SO 1999, c 14, Sched E.

49 See *Municipal Act, 2001*, SO 2001, c 25, s 238.

50 See *Local Governance Act*, SNB 2017, c 18, s 15.

51 See, for example, the City of Ottawa By-laws.

CHAPTER FOUR | **What Is Legislation Used For?**

1 [2001] 2 AC 349 at 396 (HL).

2 This is recognized in many Interpretation Acts, for example *Interpretation Act*, RSC 1985, c I-21, s 10:

> **Law always speaking**
> 10 The law shall be considered as always speaking, and where a matter or thing is expressed in the present tense, it shall be applied to the circumstances as they arise, so that effect may be given to the enactment according to its true spirit, intent and meaning.

3 See, for example, Justice Laws Website, e-Laws, or CanLII (Canadian Legal Information Institute).

4 See GD Orr, "Current Developments From Slogans to Puns: Australian Legislative Titling Revisited" (2001) 22 *Statute Law Review* 160 and P O'Brien, "Legislative Titles: What's in a Name?" *The Loophole*, November 2012.

5 There are many guides on legal research, for example, M Bueckert (ed), et al, *The Canadian Legal Research and Writing Guide*, online: 2018 CanLIIDocs 161.

6 *Re Rizzo & Rizzo Shoes Ltd*, [1998] 1 SCR 27.

7 SGG Edgar, *Craies on Statute Law*, 7th ed (London: Sweet & Maxwell, 1971) at 22.

8 See JA Corry, "The Interpretation of Statutes" in EA Driedger, *The Construction of Statutes*, 2d ed (Toronto: Butterworths, 1983) at 258ff.

9 See below, Chapter Five: How Is Legislation Understood and Applied?.

10 See below, Chapter Eight: Context — Legal Policy Presumptions.

11 RSO 1990, c E.9.

12 SO 2020, c 17.

13 About sixty-five regulations were made under the *Emergency Measures and Civil Protection Act* and thirty-seven were made under the *Reopening Ontario (A Flexible Response to COVID-19) Act*.

14 For example, O Reg 364/20 (*Rules for Areas at Step 3 and the Roadmap Exit Step*) was amended more than seventy-five times.

15 [2004] 1 SCR 76, 2004 SCC 4 at para 15.

16 *R v* Morales, [1992] SCJ No 98, [1992] 3 SCR 711. See also *O'Neill v Canada*, [2006] OJ No 4189, 82 OR (3d) 241 (SCJ).

17 See *Interpretation Act*, RSC 1985, c I-21, s 12 and *Legislation Act, 2006*, SO 2006, c 21, Sched F, s 64.

18 *Canada (Minister of Citizenship and Immigration) v Vavilov*, 2019 SCC 65.

CHAPTER FIVE | **How Is Legislation Understood and Applied?**

1 See, for example, *Inuvialuit Qitunrariit Inuuniarnikkun Maligaksat*, Inuvialuit Regional Corporation, 2021.

2 *Re Manitoba Language Rights*, [1985] 1 SCR 721 at para 46.

3 CA Allen, *Law in the Making*, 7th ed (London: Oxford University Press, London, 1964) at 435–38.

4 See JA Corry, "The Interpretation of Statutes" in EA Driedger, *The Construction of Statutes*, 2d ed (Toronto: Butterworths, 1983) at 256–57.

5 *Anon*, YB, 33-34 Edw I, 82, cited in Corry, *ibid* at 256.

6 *Craies on Statute Law*, 7th ed (London: Sweet & Maxwell, 1971) at 22.

7 See Corry, above note 4 at 258ff.

8 *Ibid* at 261.

9 *Grey v Pearson* (1857), 6 HLC 61 at 106, 10 ER 1216 at 1234.

10 Sir Henry Thring, *Practical Legislation*, 3d ed (Edinburgh: Luath Press, 2015).

11 Uniform Law Conference of Canada, "Report of the Committee on Legislative Drafting" at the first meeting of the Conference in Montreal in September 1918, online: https://ulcc-chlc.ca/Annual-Meetings/Annual-Meetings/Montreal,-QC-(6).

12 EA Driedger, "Legislative Drafting" (1949) 27 *Canadian Bar Review* 291 and EA Driedger, "The Composition of Legislation" (1953) 31 *Canadian Bar Review* 33.

13 EA Driedger, *The Composition of Legislation* (Ottawa: Queen's Printer and Controller of Stationery, 1957).

14 Most recently, see H Xanthaki, *Thornton's Legislative Drafting*, 5th ed (London: Bloomsbury Professional, 2013) and P Salembier, *Legal and Legislative Drafting*, 3d ed (Markham: Lexis Nexis Canada, 2021).

15 See M Adler, "The Plain Language Movement" in *The Oxford Handbook of Language and Law*, LM Solon & PM Tiersma (eds) (Oxford: Oxford University Press, 2012).

16 Uniform Law Conference of Canada, online: https://ulcc-chlc.ca/Civil-Section/Drafting/Drafting-Conventions.

17 EA Driedger, *The Construction of Statutes* (Toronto: Butterworths, 1976) at 67.

18 [1998] 1 SCR 27 at para 21.

19 See online: https://ulcc-chlc.ca/Civil-Section/Uniform-Acts/Model-Interpretation-Act.

20 SS 2019, c L-10.2.

21 Above note 17.

22 *Canada (Minister of Citizenship and Immigration) v Vavilov*, 2019 SCC 65 at para 118.

23 See Chapter Eight: Context.

24 See Chapter Seven: Purposes.

25 See Chapter One: What Is Drafting?

CHAPTER SIX | **Legislative Text**

1 Ruth Sullivan, *The Construction of Statutes*, 6th ed (Toronto: Lexis Nexis Canada, 2014) at 30.

2 Ruth Sullivan, *Statutory Interpretation*, 3d ed (Toronto: Irwin Law, 2016) at 61.

3 For example, the *Canadian Oxford English Dictionary*, K Barber (ed) (Don Mills, ON: Oxford University Press, 1998).

4 See, for example, *Camden (Marquis) v CIR*, [1914] KB 641 at 649–50.

5 *R v Find*, 2001 SCC 32 at para 48.

6 See, for example, *Canada (Information Commissioner) v Canada (Minister of National Defence)*, 2011 SCC 25 at para 32.

7 *Perka v The Queen*, [1984] 2 SCR 232 at 264.

8 *Ibid.*

9 See *Danby Products Ltd v Canada (Border Services Agency)*, 2021 FCA 82 at para 20, interpreting "refrigerator" in the *Customs Act*, RSC 1985, c 1 (2nd Supp).
10 *Pfizer Co Ltd v Deputy Minister of National Revenue*, [1977] 1 SCR 456 at 460.
11 *Ibid* at 460–61.
12 *Ibid*. The Court also relied on the narrower French version to reach this conclusion.
13 See, for example, *Wabush Mines v Newfoundland (Minister of Finance)* 1996 CanLII 11097 (NL CA) and *Danby*, above note 9.
14 *Unwin v Hanson*, [1891] 2 QB 115 at 119 (CA), *Granfall v Commissioners of Inland Revenue* (1876), 1 Ex D 242 at 248, and *Bombay Jewellers Ltd v The Queen*, 1998 CanLII 320 at paras 68ff (TCC).
15 *Granfall*, *ibid*.
16 See *Township of Waters v International Nickel Co of Canada*, [1959] SCR 585 and *Re Witts v British Columbia (Attorney General)* (1982), 138 DLR (3d) 555 (BCSC).
17 See *Danby*, above note 9.
18 *R v DLW*, 2016 SCC 22 at para 18.
19 *Trial Lawyers Association of British Columbia v British Columbia (Attorney General)*, 2014 SCC 59, [2014] 3 SCR 31.
20 RRO 1990, Reg 194.
21 *Short Form of Leases Act*, RSO 1990, c S.11, s 1 and *Land Registration Reform Act*, RSO 1990, c L-4, s 5.
22 See J Erasmus, "The B.C. Statute Revision Experience: 'Tax Law Rewrite on a Shoestring" *The Loophole*, June 1999. See also Alexander G Geddes, "How to Change Laws Without Changing the Law: Problems with the Presumption of Substantive Change for Plain Language Reforms" (2020) 51:1 *Ottawa Law Review* 109, 2020 CanLIIDocs 581.
23 WJV Windeyer, *Lectures on Legal History*, 2d ed (Sydney: The Law Book Company of Australasia, 1957) at 47ff.
24 *R v DLW*, 2016 SCC 22 at para 18.
25 *Will-Kare Paving & Contracting Ltd v Canada*, [2000] 1 SCR 915.
26 *Celgene Corp v Canada (Attorney General)*, [2011] SCC 1.
27 See, for example, *Interpretation Act*, RSC 1985, c I-21, s 3(1) and *Legislation Act, 2006*, SO 2006, c 21, Sched F, Part VI, s 47.
28 *R v Clay*, [2003] 3 SCR 735, 2003 SCC 75 at para 56 concluding a legislated definition of "narcotic" excluded its scientific definition.
29 Some jurisdictions have gone beyond binary gender and enacted provisions contemplating any gender: see *Legislation Act, 2006*, SO 2006, c 21, Sched F, Part VI, s 68:

> **Gender**
> **68** Gender-specific terms refer to any gender and include corporations.

30 *Interpretation Act*, RSC 1985, c I-21, s 15(2)(b).
31 SC 2019, c 28.
32 *Régie des rentes du Québec v Canada Bread Company Ltd*, 2013 SCC 46, [2013] 3 SCR 125.
33 *An Act to amend the Supplemental Pension Plans Act, the Act respecting the Québec Pension Plan and other legislative provisions*, SQ 2008, c 21, ss 1 and 20.
34 Above note 32 at para 28.
35 RSC 1985, c C-46.
36 (1993), 14 OR (3d) 682 (CA).
37 2021 SCC 30 at para 65.
38 RSC 1985, c 1 (5th Supp).
39 RSC 1985, c C-36.
40 2021 ONCA 190.
41 See the discussion above of Legal Meaning — Meaning Developed by Courts and Legal Practitioners.
42 RSBC 1996, c 163.
43 See *Abakhan & Associates Inc v Braydon Investments Ltd*, 2009 BCCA 521 at para 72.
44 RSC 1985, c 1 (5th Supp).
45 *Canada v Canada North Group Inc*, 2021 SCC 30 at para 62.
46 RSC 1985, c C-36.
47 Above note 45 at para 62.
48 (1981), 33 OR (2d) 55 (CA).
49 See *R v Gallone*, 2019 ONCA 663 at paras 29ff.
50 2006 SCC 45.
51 See *Walker v Ritchie*, *ibid* at paras 26–28.
52 *Woods (Re)*, 2021 ONCA 190 at para 48.
53 *Interpretation Act*, RSC 1985, c I-21, s 15(2)(a) and *Legislation Act, 2006*, SO 2006, c 21, Sched F, Part VI, ss 47 and 50.
54 For example, s 85 of the *Parliamentary Employment and Staff Relations Act*, RSC 1985, c 33 (2nd Supp) defines "employer" for the purposes of Part 2 (Standard Hours, Wages, Leave, Etc.) more broadly than s 3, which defines this word for the purposes of Part 1.
55 *R v Klaus*, 2021 ABCA 48 at para 39.
56 *Zeitel v Ellscheid*, [1994] 2 SCR 142 at para 152.
57 *Lukács v Canada (Transportation Agency)*, 2014 FCA 76 at paras 42–44.
58 See the discussion below of Broader Legislative Context in Chapter Eight: Context.
59 Sullivan, above note 2 at 154.
60 *R v BG*, 2021 ONSC 2299 at para 45. See *Criminal Code*, RSC 1985, c C-46, ss 278.94(2) & (3).

61 *R v BG*, *ibid* at para 46.
62 *Turgeon v Dominion Bank*, 1929 CanLII 47, [1930] SCR 67 at 71.
63 See *Re Manitoba Language Rights*, [1985] 1 SCR 721 at 774–75 and *Canadian Charter of Rights and Freedoms*, Part I of the *Constitution Act, 1982*, being Schedule B to the *Canada Act 1982* (UK), 1982, c 11, s 18 [*Charter*].
64 See *Constitution Act, 1867*, 30 & 31 Vict, c 3, s 133 (federal and Quebec), *Charter*, *ibid*, s 16 (federal and New Brunswick), and *Manitoba Act, 1870*, s 23 (Manitoba). Constitutional requirements in the *Alberta Act* and the *Saskatchewan Act* have been replaced: see *Language Act*, SS 1988-89, c L-6.1 and *Languages Act*, RSA 2000, c L-6.
65 *French Language Services Act*, RSO 1990, c F.3, *Northwest Territories Act*, SC 2014, c 2, *Yukon Act*, SC 2002, c 7, and *Nunavut Act*, SC 1993, c 28.
66 See *Official Languages Act*, SNu 2008, c 10, s 5.
67 See, for example, the land claims agreement between the Inuit of Labrador and Her Majesty in Right of Newfoundland and Labrador and Her Majesty in Right of Canada, *Labrador Inuit Land Claims Agreement Act*, SC 2005, c 27, and *Labrador Inuit Land Claims Agreement Act*, SNL 2004, c L-3.1.
68 *R v Daoust*, 2006 SCC 6.
69 For example, the French version of s 6 of the federal *Interpretation Act*, RSC 1985, c I-21 says Acts come into force "*à zéro heure à la date fixée pour son entrée en vigueur*" ("at zero hour of the day fixed for their coming into force"). The English version says they come into force "on the expiration of the previous day." These two times are functionally the same.
70 *Daoust*, above note 68.
71 *Ibid* at paras 27 and 30.
72 RSC 1985, c F-7.
73 2009 SCC 12 at para 39.

CHAPTER SEVEN | **Purposes**

1 See *Dare Human Resources Corp v Ontario (Revenue)*, 2019 ONCA 549 at para 18.
2 RSC 1985, c I-21. For an account of the historical development of interpretive approaches and the rise of purposive interpretation, see E Tucker, "The Gospel of Statutory Rules Requiring Liberal Interpretation According to St Peter's" (1985) 35 *University of Toronto Law Journal* 113.
3 EA Driedger, *The Construction of Statutes* (Toronto: Butterworths, 1976) at 67, discussed above in Chapter Five.
4 For example, in *Canada (Canadian Human Rights Commission) v Canada (Attorney General)*, 2011 SCC 53, the Court concluded that textual and contextual features of the legislation limited its scope for advancing its purposes.

5 Ruth Sullivan, *The Construction of Statutes*, 7th ed (Toronto: Lexis Nexis Canada, 2022) at 191.

6 30 & 31 Vict. c 3 (UK).

7 *Canadian Charter of Rights and Freedoms*, Part I of the *Constitution Act, 1982*, being Schedule B to the *Canada Act 1982* (UK), 1982, c 11.

8 See *Hunter v Southam*, [1984] 2 SCR 145 at 155–56.

9 *Celgene Corp v Canada (Attorney General)*, 2011 SCC 1, [2011] 1 SCR 3.

10 *John Doe v Ontario (Finance)*, 2014 SCC 36 at paras 41–46.

11 See *Canada Trustco Mortgage Co v Canada*, [2005] SCC 54 at para 47 and *Ted Leroy Trucking Ltd v HMTQ*, 2007 BCSC 191 at paras 21–22.

12 RSO 1990, c H.8.

13 See, for example, the *Broadcasting Act*, SC 1991, c 11, s 3 and the *Accessible Canada Act*, SC 2019, c 10, s 6.

14 *John Doe v Ontario (Finance)*, 2014 SCC 36 at paras 41–46. See also *Shergar Development Inc v Windsor (City)*, 2020 ONCA 490 at paras 31–33 discussing the multiple purposes of providing adequate compensation for expropriated property, but also encouraging settlement of compensation disputes and *Woods (Re)*, 2021 ONCA 190 balancing protection of the public and fairness to a person found not criminally responsible for their conduct.

15 See, for example, *R v Appulonappa*, 2015 SCC 59 at para 34.

16 SO 1996, c 2, Sched A.

17 2013 SCC 53, [2013] 3 SCR 341.

18 *Ibid* at para 50.

19 *Ibid* at para 155.

20 See, for example, the *Accessible Canada Act*, SC 2019, c 10, s 5:

> 5 The purpose of this Act is to benefit all persons, especially persons with disabilities, through the realization, within the purview of matters coming within the legislative authority of Parliament, of a Canada without barriers, on or before January 1, 2040, particularly by the identification and removal of barriers, and the prevention of new barriers, in the following areas:
>
> (a) employment;
> (b) the built environment;
> (c) information and communication technologies;
> (c.1) communication, other than information and communication technologies;
> (d) the procurement of goods, services and facilities;
> (e) the design and delivery of programs and services;
> (f) transportation; and
> (g) areas designated under regulations made under paragraph 117(1)(b).

See also Kent Roach, "The Uses and Audiences of Preambles in Legislation" (2001) 47 *McGill Law Journal* 129.

21 See *Interpretation Act*, RSC 1985, c I-21, s 13.

22 See, for example, *R v Appulonappa*, 2015 SCC 59 at para 34.

CHAPTER EIGHT | **Context**

1 *Monsanto Canada Inc v Ontario (Superintendent of Financial Services)*, [2004] 3 SCR 152, 2004 SCC 54 at para 35.

2 See, for example, *AG v Prince Ernest Augustus of Hanover*, [1957] AC 436 (HL) 436 at 463:

> [T]he elementary rule must be observed that no one should profess to understand any part of a statute . . . before he has read the whole of it. Until he has done so he is not entitled to say that it or any part of it is clear and unambiguous.

3 A Fraser, G Birch & W Dawson, *Beauchesne's Rules and Forms of the House of Commons of Canada*, 5th ed (Toronto: Carswell Co Ltd, 1978) at 220.

4 See *Legislation Act, 2006*, SO 2006, c 21, Sched F, s 70.

5 See M Bosc & A Gagnon, *House of Commons Procedure and Practice*, 3d ed (Ottawa: House of Commons, 2017) c 16 —The Legislative Process — Structure of Bills — Headings.

6 See Ruth Sullivan, *Statutory Interpretation*, 3d ed (Toronto: Irwin Law, 2016) at 161.

7 1985 CanLII 2652 (Sask CA).

8 See also the discussion of Implied Exclusion above in Chapter Six: Legislative Text.

9 2014 SCC 67 at para 92.

10 *Lévis (City) v Fraternité des policiers de Lévis Inc*, 2007 SCC 14 at para 47.

11 RSC 1985, c 31 (4th Supp).

12 RSC 1985, c C-26, s 2.

13 RSO 1990, c O.2.

14 SO 2002, c 30, Sched A.

15 2018 ONCA 313.

16 *Ibid* at para 52.

17 *Ibid* at paras 59–64.

18 *Ibid* at paras 65–73. See also the discussion of consequential analysis below in Chapter Nine: Application.

19 See, for example, *R v Schmidt*, [1987] 1 SCR 500 where the later general rule about appeals to the Supreme Court was applied to override the earlier more

specific rule prohibiting appeals. Parliament then amended the specific rule to eliminate the conflict (see SC 1990, c 8, s 36).

20 See *Conseil scolaire francophone de la ColombieBritannique v British Columbia*, 2013 SCC 42 (CanLII), [2013] 2 SCR 774 at para 44.

21 See, for example, *Lévis (City) v Fraternité des policiers de Lévis Inc*, 2007 SCC 14 at paras 85–90.

22 The Conference's website can be accessed online: https://ulcc-chlc.ca.

23 2011 SCC 53, [2011] 3 SCR 471.

24 RSC 1985, c H-6.

25 *Declaration on the Rights of Indigenous Peoples Act*, SBC 2019, c 44 and *United Nations Declaration on the Rights of Indigenous Peoples Act*, SC 2021, c 14.

26 SNWT 1994, c 26 and SNWT 1994 (Nu), c 26.

27 *Constitution Act, 1982*, Sched B to the *Canada Act 1982* (UK), 1982, c 11, s 52 and the schedule identify some of the legislative components of the Constitution. The Supreme Court of Canada has also identified other elements, notably constitutional principles: see *Reference re Secession of Quebec*, [1998] 2 SCR 217 and Parliamentary Privilege: see *Mikisew Cree First Nation v Canada (Governor General in Council)*, 2018 SCC 40.

28 30 & 31 Vict, c 3 (UK).

29 Part I of the *Constitution Act, 1982*, being Schedule B to the *Canada Act 1982* (UK), 1982, c 11.

30 *Canada Act 1982* (UK), c 11, Sched B; *Constitution Act, 1982*, Part 1.

31 See *Reference re Secession of Quebec*, [1998] 2 SCR 217.

32 *Constitution Act, 1982*, s 52(1).

33 See *R v Sharpe*, [2001] SCJ No 3 at para 33 where McLachlin J said:

> Supplementing [Driedger's modern] approach is the presumption that Parliament *intended* to enact legislation in conformity with the *Charter*. . . . *If a legislative provision can be read both in a way that is constitutional and in a way that is not, the former reading should be adopted.* [Emphasis added.]

34 RSC 1985, c C-46.

35 2012 SCC 47.

36 *Bell ExpressVu Limited Partnership v Rex*, [2002] SCC 42 at para 62.

37 See *Wilson v British Columbia (Superintendent of Motor Vehicles)*, 2015 SCC 47 at para 20, [2015] 3 SCR 300. See also JM Keyes & C Diamond, "Constitutional Inconsistency in Legislation — Interpretation and the Ambiguous Role of Ambiguity" (2017), 48 *Ott L Rev* 315.

38 See *Mitchell v Minister of National Revenue*, 2001 SCC 33 at para 9.

39 For a general description of these traditions, see J Borrows, *Canada's Indigenous Constitution* (University of Toronto Press: Toronto, 2010) at 72–77.

40 See, for example, Donald A Grinde & Bruce E Johansen, *Exemplar of Liberty: Native American and the Evolution of Democracy* (Los Angeles: American Indian Studies Center, University of California, 1991).

41 See *Mitchell v Minister of National Revenue*, 2001 SCC 33 at para 10.

42 See Government of Canada, *Implementation of Modern Treaties and Self-Government Agreements, July 2015–March 2018 Provisional Annual Report* (Ottawa: 2019).

43 *Mitchell v Peguis Indian Band*, [1990] 2 SCR 85 at 143. See also a recent affirmation of this approach in *Restoule v Canada (Attorney General)*, 2021 ONCA 779 at paras 105ff.

44 *Ibid*. Note, however, the dissent of Dickson CJ at 99.

45 (2004), 184 OAC 84 at 94 and RSO 1990, c C 38.

46 *Declaration on the Rights of Indigenous Peoples Act*, SBC 2019, c 44 and *United Nations Declaration on the Rights of Indigenous Peoples Act*, SC 2021, c 14.

47 Above note 22.

48 RSC 1985, c C-46, ss. 8(3).

49 *Ibid*, Part 9.

50 *R v DLW*, 2016 SCC 22 at para 14. See also *Kazemi v Islamic Republic of Iran*, 2014 SCC 62 at para 54.

51 *Canada (Attorney General) v Thouin*, 2017 SCC 46 at para 19.

52 *R v DLW*, above note 50 at para 21.

53 RSO 1990, c O.2 [emphasis added] discussed in *MacKay v Starbucks Corporation*, 2017 ONCA 350 at para 10. Also see *Kazemi v Islamic Republic of Iran*, above note 50 at para 58, finding that a codification of customary international law relating to state immunity was accomplished by s 3 of the *State Immunity Act*, RSC 1985, c S-18:

> 3. (1) Except as provided by this Act, a foreign state is immune from the jurisdiction of any court in Canada.

54 As in *R v DLW*, above note 50.

55 *Rawluk v Rawluk*, [1990] 1 SCR 70.

56 LQ 1991, c 64.

57 See P-A Côté & M Devinat, *Interprétation des loi*, 5e éd (Cowansville: Les Éditions Thémis, 2021) at 388.

58 For example, subsection 14.06(2) of the *Bankruptcy and Insolvency Act*, RSC 1985, c B-3 referring to "the trustee's gross negligence or wilful misconduct or, in the Province of Quebec, the trustee's gross or intentional fault."

59 For example, "legal counsel/conseiller juridique" in the *Bankruptcy and Insolvency Act*, RSC 1985, c B-3, which encompasses advocates and notaries in Quebec and barristers and solicitors in common law provinces and territories.

60 RSC 1985, c I-21. See also s 8.1.

61 *Aboriginal Custom Adoption Recognition Act*, SNWT 1994, c 26.

62 *Nevsun Resources Ltd v Araya*, 2020 SCC 5 at paras 86 and 95.

63 *Ibid* at para 77.

64 See, for example, the *Wrecked, Abandoned or Hazardous Vessels Act*, SC 2019, c 1, s 50(1).

65 United Nations, *Treaty Series*, vol 1155, at 331, Part III, Section 3.

66 See, for example, the *Anti-personnel Mines Convention*, SC 1997, c 33.

67 *R v Hape*, [2007] 2 SCR 292 at para 53.

68 *Ibid.*

69 *Kazemi v Islamic Republic of Iran*, above note 50 at para 63.

70 See, for example, *R v Zora*, 2020 SCC 14 applying the presumption that subjective intent is required to convict for serious offences.

71 See *Pong Marketing and Promotions Inc v Ontario Media Development Corp*, 2018 ONCA 555 at para 41.

72 See *Shergar Development Inc v Windsor (City)*, 2020 ONCA 490 at para 34.

73 See *Baker v Canada (Minister of Citizenship and Immigration)*, [1999] 2 SCR 817 at para 20 and *Craft Acquisitions Corp v Toronto (City)*, 2019 ONSC 3636 at para 46.

74 See *Alberta (Information and Privacy Commissioner) v University of Calgary*, 2016 SCC 53.

75 See *Abrahams v Attorney General of Canada*, [1983] 1 SCR 2 at 10 and *Re Rizzo & Rizzo Shoes Ltd*, [1998] 1 SCR 27 at para 36.

76 See, for example, *Bell ExpressVu Limited Partnership v Rex*, [2002] SCC 42 at para 28 and *Wood v CTS of Canada Co*, 2018 ONCA 758 at para 77. See generally T Cromwell, S Anstis & T Touchie, "Revisiting the Role of Presumptions of Legislative Intent in Statutory Interpretation" (2017) 95 *Canadian Bar Review* 297.

77 *Agricultural Credit Corp of Saskatchewan v Novak* (1985), 134 Sask R 87, CanLII 3982 (CA).

78 *R v ADH*, 2013 SCC 28 at para 83.

79 *R v Ipeelee*, 2012 SCC 13 at para 62.

80 *Canada (Canadian Human Rights Commission) v Canada (Attorney General)*, 2011 SCC 53, [2011] 3 SCR 471 at para 43.

81 See, for example, *R v Jacob*, 2009 ONCA 73 at para 43.

82 See, for example, the *Legislative Revision and Consolidation Act*, RSC 1985, c S-20 and *Statutes Revision Act, 1989*, SO 1989, c 81.

83 [1986] 3 FC 3 (CA).

84 *Ibid* at 10.

85 *Canada (Canadian Human Rights Commission) v Canada (Attorney General)*, above note 80 at para 44.

86 *Ibid* at paras 46–52.

87 RSC 1985, c H-6.

88 *Ibid* at para 44.

89 [1998] 1 SCR 27 at para 35.
90 See *Amateur Youth Soccer Association v Canada (Revenue Agency)*, [2007] 3 SCR 217, 2007 SCC 42 at para 12.
91 *Re Rizzo & Rizzo Shoes Ltd*, above note 75 at para 35. See also *Celgene Corp v Canada (Attorney General)*, 2011 SCC 1 at paras 26–28.
92 See *Telecommunications Employees Association of Manitoba Inc v Manitoba Telecom Services Inc*, 2014 SCC 11 at paras 70–74.
93 RSO 1990, c O.2.
94 Ontario Law Reform Commission, *Report on Occupiers' Liability* (Toronto: Department of Justice, 1972).
95 Model Acts are published on the website of the Uniform Law Conference, online: www.ulcc-chlc.ca.
96 RSS 1978, c C-31.
97 2019 SKCA 18.
98 *Ibid* at para 44.
99 See, for example, *British Columbia Human Rights Tribunal v Schrenk*, 2017 SCC 62 at paras 65 and 130.
100 See *Canada (Information Commissioner) v Canada (Attorney General)*, 2015 FC 405 at para 29.
101 See *Canada (Attorney General) v Bedford*, 2013 SCC 72 at para 42.
102 See *Flieger v New Brunswick*, [1993] 2 SCR 651 at 659.
103 *Canada (Minister of Citizenship and Immigration) v Vavilov*, 2019 SCC 65 at para 118.
104 *Cuthbertson v Rasouli*, 2013 SCC 53, [2013] 3 SCR 341 at para 69.
105 *Monsanto Canada Inc v Ontario (Superintendent of Financial Services)*, [2004] 3 SCR 152 at para 35.
106 *Amateur Youth Soccer Association v Canada (Revenue Agency)*, above note 90 at para 10.

CHAPTER NINE | **Application**

1 See Ruth Sullivan, *Statutory Interpretation*, 3d ed (Toronto: Irwin Law, 2016) at 287 citing *Canada (Information Commissioner) v Canada (Minister of Defence)*, 2011 SCC 25 at para 40.
2 *Godbout v Pagé*, 2017 SCC 18.
3 *Ibid* at para 72. Note, however, that the Ontario Court of Appeal in *Goldsmith v National Bank of Canada*, 2016 ONCA 22 at para 37 suggests plausibility depends on purposes and context as well as the text. This arguably distorts the notion of plausibility as a factor related to the text.
4 *Goldsmith*, *ibid* at para 38.
5 *Re Vabalis* (1983), 43 OR (2d) 609 (CA).

6 *Felippa v Canada (Citizenship and Immigration)*, 2011 FCA 272.

7 RSC 1985, c F-7.

8 See *ATCO Gas & Pipeline Ltd v Alberta (Energy & Utilities Board)*, 2006 SCC 4 at para 51.

9 See, for example, *R v McIntosh*, [1995] 1 SCR 686 at 701 and *R v Myers*, 2019 SCC 18 at para 33.

10 In *Re Rizzo and Rizzo Shoes Ltd*, [1998] 1 SCR 27 at para 27, the Supreme Court described absurdity as follows:

> According to Côté, *supra*, an interpretation can be considered absurd if it leads to ridiculous or frivolous consequences, if it is extremely unreasonable or inequitable, if it is illogical or incoherent, or if it is incompatible with other provisions or with the object of the legislative enactment (at pp. 378-80). Sullivan echoes these comments noting that a label of absurdity can be attached to interpretations which defeat the purpose of a statute or render some aspect of it pointless or futile (Sullivan, *Construction of Statutes*, *supra*, at p. 88).

11 See *Re Rizzo and Rizzo Shoes Ltd*, *ibid* at para 29, finding the result of applying the appellant's interpretation would result in a distinction between employees terminated before their employer's bankruptcy and those terminated afterward.

12 See *R v Clay*, 2003 SCC 75 at para 49.

13 See *R v Monney*, [1999] 1 SCR 652 at para 28 and *R v Quesnelle*, 2014 SCC 46 at para 56.

14 See *Cuthbertson v Rasouli*, 2013 SCC 53, [2013] 3 SCR 341 at paras 57–58.

15 *Skoke-Graham v The Queen*, [1985] 1 SCR 106.

16 See Sullivan, above note 1 at 216ff, citing *R v Paré*, [1987] 2 SCR 618.

17 Sullivan, *ibid* at 220–21.

18 *Perka v The Queen*, [1984] 2 SCR 232 at 264 and RSC 1970, c N-1.

19 *Ibid* at 264–66.

20 *Ibid* at 265–66.

21 *Edwards v Canada (Attorney General)*, [1930] AC 124 (PC) and 30 & 31 Vict, c 3 (UK).

22 *Ibid* at para 44.

23 See *Hunter et al v Southam Inc*, [1984] 2 SCR 145 at 155 and *Reference re Senate Reform*, 2014 SCC 32 at para 25.

24 2009 ONCA 151 at para 29, citing Ruth Sullivan, *Sullivan and Driedger on the Construction of Statutes*, 4th ed (Markham: LexisNexis Canada, 2002) at 113.

25 RSC 1985, c 34.

26 See *Rogers Communication Inc v Society of Composers, Authors and Music Publishers of Canada*, [2012] SCC 35 at para 39.

27 2021 ONCA 190 at para 44.

28 See *Craies on Statute Law*, 7th ed (London: Sweet & Maxwell, 1971) at 383.

29 See, for example, *Interpretation Act*, RSC 1985, c I-21, s 5 and *Legislation Act, 2006*, SO 2006, c 21, Sched F, Part VI, s 47, ss 8–9.

30 SC 2013, c 33.

31 See *Criminal Law Amendment Act, Reference*, [1970] SCR 777.

32 See *Statutes Repeal Act*, SC 2008, c 20; *Statute Repeal Act*, SNB 2012, c 13; *Statutes Repeal Act*, SA 2013, c S-19.3; *Legislation Act, 2006*, SO 2006, c 21, Sched F, Part VI, s 10.1.

33 RSC 1985, c C-8.

34 RSC 1985, c S-22, s 9.

35 SO 2006, c 21, Sched F, Part VI, ss.22(2).

36 CQLR c R-18.1, s 18.

37 See *Statutory Instruments Act*, RSC 1985, c S-22, s 9; *Legislation Act, 2006*, SO 2006, c 21, Sched F, Part VI, s 22(2) and *Regulations Act*, CQLR c R-18.1, s 19.

38 See *Tran v Canada (Public Safety and Emergency Preparedness)*, 2017 SCC 50 at para 44 [*Tran*].

39 See *British Columbia v Imperial Tobacco Canada Ltd*, 2005 SCC 49 at para 69 and *Canadian Charter of Rights and Freedoms*, Part I of the *Constitution Act, 1982*, being Schedule B to the *Canada Act 1982* (UK), 1982, c 11, s 11(g) and (i). Note, however, that these provisions can be overridden under s 33 of the *Charter*. This has never been done.

40 See *Tran* above note 38 at paras 48–49.

41 See *Dikranian v Quebec (Attorney General)*, 2005 SCC 73 at paras 37–40.

42 See, for example, *Interpretation Act*, RSC 1985, c I-21, ss 43–44 and *Legislation Act, 2006*, SO 2006, c 21, Sched F, Part VI, ss 51–52.

43 SC 1990, c 43, Ss 64(2). The constitutionality of this provision was upheld in *Authorson v Canada*, 2003 SCC 39. For further examples, see *Green Energy Repeal Act, 2018*, SO 2018, c 16, ss 8(10) adding s 70.9 to the *Planning Act*, RSO 1990, c P.13. See also above Chapter One: What Is Drafting? — Provisions and Their Arrangement.

44 See *Lin v Weng*, 2022 ONCA 367 at paras 26–27. See also Ruth Sullivan, *Interpretation of Legislation*, 3d ed (Irwin Law: Toronto: 2016) at 346–50.

45 See *CI Mutual Funds Inc v Canada*, [1999] 2 FC 613 (FCA).

46 See *Régie des rentes du Québec v Canada Bread Co*, 2013 SCC 46 at para 28.

47 See *Brosseau v Alberta Securities Commission*, [1989] 1 SCR 301 at 321. But note the restrictive interpretation of this exception in *Tran*, above note 38 at paras 47–50.

48 *Application under s 83.28 of Criminal Code*, 2004 SCC 42. But note the debate over what constitutes a procedural matter in *R v Chouhan*, 2021 SCC 26 at paras 91–103 and 170–75.

49 See *Tran*, above note 38 at para 50.
50 This presumption is expressed in *Interpretation Act*, RSC 1985, c I-21, s 8(1).
51 See, for example, *City of Toronto Act, 2006*, SO 2006, c 11, Sched A and *City of Ottawa Act, 1999*, SO 1999, c 14, Sched E.
52 See *Society of Composers, Authors and Music Publishers of Canada v Canadian Association of Internet Providers* [*SOCAN*], 2004 SCC 45 at para 54 in relation to the federal Parliament.
53 See *R v Hape*, 2007 SCC 26 at paras 40ff.
54 See *1068754 Alberta Ltd v Québec (Agence du revenu)*, 2019 SCC 37 at para 92.
55 *Ibid* at para 86.
56 See *SOCAN*, above note 52 at para 54.
57 See for example *Aeronautics Act*, RSC 1985, c A-2, s 4 and *Canada Shipping Act*, SC 2001, c 26, s 8.
58 SC 1996, c 31, s 9.
59 See *Craies on Statute Law*, 7th ed (London: Sweet & Maxwell, 1971) at 423.
60 RSC 1985, c I-21. See also *Legislation Act, 2006*, SO 2006, c 21, Sched F, Part VI, s 71.
61 See, for example, *Canadian Environmental Protection Act, 1999*, SC 1999, c 33, s 5.
62 See *Interpretation Act*, RSBC 1996, c 238, s 14 and *Interpretation Act*, RSPEI 1988, c I-8, s 14.
63 See *Friends of the Oldman River Society v Canada (Minister of Transport)*, [1992] 1 SCR 3 at 60–61.
64 See *Sparling v Quebec (Caisse de dépôt et de placement du Québec)*, [1988] 2 SCR 1015.

ANNEX 1 | The Uniform Law Conference of Canada Drafting Conventions

1 Online: www.ulcc-chlc.ca/Civil-Section/Drafting/Drafting-Conventions . Reproduced with the permission of the Uniform Law Conference of Canada.

ANNEX 2 | The Uniform Law Conference of Canada Model Interpretation Act

1 Online: www.ulcc-chlc.ca/ULCC/media/EN-Uniform-Acts/Model-Interpretation-Act.pdf. Reproduced with the permission of the Uniform Law Conference of Canada.

Useful Websites

CanLII (Canadian Legal Information Institute): www.canlii.org/en
CanLII provides free online access to legislation of every jurisdiction in Canada (federal, provincial, and territorial) and to decisions of Canadian courts and legal commentary.

Uniform Law Conference of Canada: www.ulcc-chlc.ca
The Uniform Law Conference of Canada is the oldest law reform body in the country and plays a key role in developing uniform legislation in civil and commercial matters and in proposing changes to the criminal law. Its website contains model uniform Acts as well as conventions and principles for drafting legislation.

Uniform Law Conference of Canada Drafting Conventions:
www.ulcc-chlc.ca/Civil-Section/Drafting/Drafting-Conventions

Uniform Law Conference of Canada Model Interpretation Act:
www.ulcc-chlc.ca/Civil-Section/Uniform-Acts/
Model-Interpretation-Act

LEGISinfo: www.parl.ca/legisinfo
LEGISinfo provides information regarding legislation before Parliament, including the full text of the most recent version of a bill and any previous versions of the bill. It also includes all bills from previous sessions going back to the 37th Parliament in 2001.

Federal and Provincial Laws

- **Justice Canada:** laws-lois.justice.gc.ca/eng
- **Alberta:** www.alberta.ca/laws-online-catalogue.aspx
- **British Columbia:** www.bclaws.gov.bc.ca
- **Manitoba:** https://web2.gov.mb.ca/laws/index.php
- **New Brunswick:** www2.gnb.ca/content/gnb/en/departments/public-safety/attorney-general/content/acts_regulations.html
- **Newfoundland and Labrador:** www.assembly.nl.ca/legislation/sr/titleindex.htm
- **Northwest Territories:** www.justice.gov.nt.ca/en/legislation
- **Nova Scotia:** https://novascotia.ca/just/acts.asp
- **Nunavut:** www.nunavutlegislation.ca/en
- **Ontario:** www.ontario.ca/laws
- **Prince Edward Island:** www.princeedwardisland.ca/en/legislation/all/all/a
- **Quebec:** www.legisquebec.gouv.qc.ca/en
- **Saskatchewan:** https://publications.saskatchewan.ca/#/freelaw
- **Yukon:** https://laws.yukon.ca/cms/

Commonwealth Association of Legislative Counsel (CALC): www.calc.ngo

Commonwealth Secretariat, Commonwealth of Learning Training Materials on Legislative Drafting: https://oasis.col.org/items/72b2efae-7883-44da-89ff-75226c052dd0

Index

About the Authors

Wendy Gordon holds a BA Hons in English literature from Western University and an LLB from Queen's University. She was called to the Ontario Bar in 1987. Wendy was legislative counsel at the Department of Justice for nineteen years and at the House of Commons in the Office of the Law Clerk for ten years, culminating in the position of Deputy Law Clerk, Legislation Services. As legislative counsel, Wendy advised on complex federal statutes and regulations, drafted bills and amendments for Members of Parliament, and provided advice on diverse legislative matters falling under federal jurisdiction. Wendy developed and piloted plain language regulatory initiatives at the Department of Justice, developed and taught courses at the Canada School of Public Service, and has been a frequent guest lecturer at the law schools of McGill University and the University of Ottawa.

Wendy is a member of the Canadian Institute for the Administration of Justice and the Commonwealth Association of Legislative Counsel (CALC). Within CALC, Wendy held the position of regional representative for the Americas and is on the editorial board of *The Loophole*, the CALC journal about the preparation and enactment of legislation.

John Mark Keyes is a sessional professor at the Faculty of Law, University of Ottawa, and an instructor in the Legislative Drafting Program of Athabasca University. He has an LLB from the University of Toronto and a Diploma in Legislative Drafting and an LLM from the University of Ottawa.

Professor Keyes was previously legislative counsel in the Department of Justice (Canada) drafting regulations and government bills. He later occupied various managerial positions and was the Chief Legislative Counsel from 2005 until 2013. He has also written many academic articles and a monograph, *Executive Legislation*, the third edition of which was published by Lexis Nexis in 2021.

About the Editor

Gregory Tardi, BCL, LLB, DJur, is the general editor of the Understanding Canada Collection. He is a member of the Barreau du Québec and serves both as president of the Institute of Parliamentary and Political Law and as editor of the *Journal of Parliamentary and Political Law*. He has served as legal counsel with Elections Canada and at the House of Commons. He has taught at McGill, York, and Queen's universities and is the author of several books, including *The Theory and Practice of Political Law* and *Anatomy of an Election*.

Printed and bound by CPI Group (UK) Ltd, Croydon, CR0 4YY

30/06/2026

14910916-0002